T0306031

"As a Chief Enterprise Architect with decades of experience steering technology strategies for industry giants like Intuit and Veritas, I found this book to be a trail-blazing compass for traditional companies and modern startups alike. Its insightful navigation through the evolution of data, AI and advanced analytics, combined with actionable frameworks for technical and organisational implementation to embed advanced analytics, comes together seamlessly as a strategy playbook for cultivating a culture of data-driven excellence. A must-read for any leader harnessing the dynamic potential of advanced analytics!"
—**Geeta Pyne**, *Chief Architect at TIAA*

"This is a timely guide that deeply aligns with my own experience with technology and software business! As the CEO and co-founder of Weaviate, I've witnessed firsthand the pivotal role that data, AI, and analytics play in guiding informed decision-making and shaping the trajectory of businesses. In an era where AI and machine learning are increasingly integral to most businesses, this book couldn't have come at a more opportune moment. Many would stand to benefit from the clear roadmap that Ferris and Tan have laid out to navigate the complexities of modern analytics!"
—**Bob van Luijt**, *CEO and Co-Founder of Weaviate*

"I loved this book. It covers the whole gambit from describing what advanced analytics is through to how to drive value from your analytics investment. It also talks about the more defensive parts of a data strategy—building firm foundations and governance and ethics. It's essentially a playbook for building a data strategy and culture in a modern but traditional organisation."
—**Andy Sutton**, *General Manager, Advanced Analytics, Endeavour Group*

"Simplifying and conveying topics that are multi-generational, systemic and cross-discipline is not for the faint of heart. Yet somehow accomplished in this important body of work. Walking that fine line between being comprehensive yet pragmatic, it is a must-read for anyone seeking real-world examples of what must be built right with data, analytics and AI foundations or what can go very wrong without this basis. There is nothing quite like people who have 'been there, done that', to create an engaging roadmap and narrative focused on value and genuine engagement first."
—**Valerie A. Logan**, *CEO and Founder, The Data Lodge (Your Home for Data Literacy)*

"If you are looking for a guide to empower you with your data and analytical work and to hone your knowledge on creating action with data and analytics, then turn to Jason Tan and Brian Ferris's book. Don't miss out on this opportunity to further your knowledge on these important matters."
—**Jordan Morrow**, *Senior Vice President of Data and AI Transformation, AgileOn*

Transition to Advanced Analytics

Amazon knows the products we're interested in and shows us more to boost the size of our shopping cart. Google Maps knows the best route to get from A to B and recommends it to get us there in the shortest possible time. Netflix knows the media we enjoy most and recommends more to boost streaming time. However, many companies still fall short with their data analytics practices.

This book focuses on how to embed advanced analytics directly into daily business operations and complement an enterprise system. This book can guide you in how traditional industries like retailers, banks and insurers can utilise and develop advanced analytics complementing their enterprise systems while embedding advanced analytics directly to optimise revenue and customer experience. Detailed in this book is a world-class analytics application used by loyalty point providers, banks, insurers and leading retailers.

The title also provides a step-by-step implementation framework for Chief Digital and Artificial Intelligence Offices to develop their advanced analytics capabilities in tandem with legacy IT systems.

Jason Tan is the owner of DDA Labs and *The Analytics Show* (*TAS*) podcast. Together with his team, they develop and embed analytics into business operations to optimise results for insurers and financial service companies. At *TAS*, Jason interviews top business leaders worldwide on using data science to run a high-performing modern organisation. The goal behind *TAS* is to help data and analytics leaders break through barriers and get out of their shells to have their voices heard confidently. Through the podcast, listeners and guests alike are able to attain the skills needed for delivering business benefits through data.

Brian Ferris is the Chief Data and Technology Officer at Loyalty New Zealand, leading the data, analytics and technology teams. Loyalty New Zealand runs New Zealand's most loved loyalty programme – Flybuys – as well as the Lab360 precision marketing team. Over the past four years, the teams have completed an agile transformation and a full migration to the cloud, decommissioning the legacy data centres. In addition, the data management and precision marketing stacks have been completely revamped with artificial intelligence and machine learning tooling in a flexible modern architecture. Prior to Loyalty NZ, Brian ran Enterprise Data and Analytics for Nike in Europe, the Middle East and Africa, and before that, he held senior data and analytics roles at Heineken, BAT and the European Central Bank. Brian's focus through all of his roles has been transforming people and cultures to deliver real business value from the data assets.

Transition to Advanced Analytics

Get a Return on Your Analytics Investment

Jason Tan and Brian Ferris

CRC Press
Taylor & Francis Group
Boca Raton London New York

CRC Press is an imprint of the
Taylor & Francis Group, an **informa** business

A CHAPMAN & HALL BOOK

First edition published 2024
by CRC Press
2385 NW Executive Center Drive, Suite 320, Boca Raton FL 33431

and by CRC Press
4 Park Square, Milton Park, Abingdon, Oxon, OX14 4RN

CRC Press is an imprint of Taylor & Francis Group, LLC
© 2024 Jason Tan and Brian Ferris

ISBN: 978-1-032-52755-0 (hbk)
ISBN: 978-1-032-52754-3 (pbk)
ISBN: 978-1-003-40822-2 (ebk)

DOI: 10.1201/9781003408222

Contents

Acknowledgements

Jason and I would like to acknowledge the help and support of our communications support, Christine Adair, in making this book possible. My and Jason's careers have given us a deep knowledge of advanced analytics, but they did not prepare us for our first foray into writing a book. Christine was invaluable in helping us take our raw draft and shape it into the finished product you have in front of you. Her experience and skills from a long career in communications and media allowed her to take what we had said and mould it into what we meant.

Preface

In today's rapidly evolving technological landscape, investment in advanced analytics is reaching unprecedented heights across the globe. Large and mid-sized corporations, as well as government departments, are increasingly recognising the potential of leveraging data for informed decision-making and strategic advantage. Despite this burgeoning interest, a staggering 85% of advanced analytics projects fail, as reported by Gartner. This alarming statistic resonates with the personal experiences of both of us, having witnessed numerous projects, brimming with potential, culminate in costly failures and unfulfilled promises.

Our journey, as practitioners and executives, has traversed various scales of projects and organisations, ranging from nimble startups to expansive corporations. This diverse experience has afforded us a unique vantage point to discern the patterns of success and failure in the realm of advanced analytics. We have gleaned invaluable insights and practical strategies that have consistently proven instrumental in steering projects towards their intended objectives. This book is a distillation of these learnings, shared with the aspiration to illuminate the path for organisations embarking on their own advanced analytics journey.

In the burgeoning era of Generative AI, the significance of AI and advanced analytics is poised to reach new zeniths. The transformative potential of these technologies underscores the imperative for organisations to adeptly navigate the transition to an analytics-centric paradigm. This conviction forms the bedrock of our endeavour in authoring this book, aiming to equip readers with pragmatic tips and strategies for a seamless and successful transition to the future of advanced analytics.

"Transition to Advanced Analytics: Get Return for Your Analytics Investment" unfolds in three comprehensive parts:

1. **Part 1** (Chapter 1 - 3) delves into the contrasting landscapes of traditional companies and modern startups in the context of software and
advanced analytics utilisation. It offers our perspectives on the distinct
approaches how traditional companies could adopt, both in the present
and the impending future, to effectively harness the power of advanced
analytics.

2. **Part 2** (Chapter 4) is dedicated to the technical implementation of
advanced analytics. It provides a deep dive into our proven approaches and
suggestions to ensure the success of advanced analytics projects. A segment is devoted to elucidating the concept of embedded advanced analytics, illustrated through a real-world Generative AI project, offering readers
a tangible and relatable insight into technical implementation strategies.

3. **Part 3** (Chapter 5 - 12) shifts the focus to the organisational implementation of advanced analytics. Beyond the technical realm, the success of
advanced analytics projects is inextricably linked to various organisational
facets. This section presents various frameworks and strategies to ensure
successful project delivery, addressing the organisational dimensions that
play a crucial role in the fruition of advanced analytics initiatives.

In the pages that follow, embark on a comprehensive exploration of the
world of advanced analytics. Arm yourself with the knowledge and
insights shared, and stride confidently towards a future where the promises of advanced analytics are not just envisioned, but realised to their full-
est potential.

Welcome to the journey towards a successful transition to advanced
analytics.

Brian Ferris and Jason Tan

Foreword

On the 6th May 2017, the cover of The Economist hailed the world's most valuable resource was no longer oil, but data. The leader was a call for a new approach to anti-trust laws surrounding the use of data by technology titans like Alphabet, Amazon, Apple, Facebook (now Meta) and Microsoft.

But in a special report just three years later, The Economist revisited the oil / data metaphor, acknowledging that "like oil, data must be refined to be useful".

Once extracted and refined, oil drives the consumer and business economy. It facilitates our weekly trips to the supermarket, or our shopping being deliver to us from websites, via ships, planes and trucks. In business markets, has the lowering of trade barriers facilitated the freer transportation/movement of goods and services (and thus globalisation), or has our ability to transport goods around the world lowered trade barriers (a classic "chicken and egg" conundrum)?

And yes, while acknowledging that oil is also a fossil fuel which we need to use less of if we are to stabilise temperature rises below 1.5deg C to reach net zero, it is worthwhile continuing with the oil / data metaphor.

The book you are holding in your hands, or reading on your device, is the key to extracting and refining your 'oil' (i.e., your data) to get it powering your business, regardless of whether you are in the B2B, B2C or some other space.

I couldn't think of two better authors than Brian and Jason to write this book. Both have gold-plated CVs in field of data and analytics, but in different realms within that field. They capitalise on this by assembling individually written chapters of this book, but collectively they form one of the best data and analytics playbooks on the market.

The book certainly pulls no punches, diving straight into the world of Artificial Intelligence as early as the first paragraph of chapter 1. Over the course of the following 12 chapters, it covers everything that both traditional and modern start-ups companies need to know about data and advanced analytics.

No stone is left unturned and no topic is off the cards: it's all here, in both depth and breadth. When you turn this page, you'll start a journey through everything to do with data and analytics, including (bit not limited to) the role and importance of change mindsets, communication, collaboration and co-creation, the role of a CDAO or Chief Data & Analytic Officer (who knew?), the development of business cases and getting them over the line, corporate governance ethics and privacy. You will also read about the challenges associated with migrations from legacy systems (a challenge in any field, not just data and analytics!), and the authors clear language brings clarity to terms like cosine similarity, Euclidean distances, and vector embedding.

This book draws on real life experiences and case studies from the coalface of data and analytics. It is useful for executing your first data and analytics project right through to fine tuning the projects of seasoned data and analytics professionals, ultimately delivering tangible economic value to any organisation that adopts the guidance herein.

Jon Manning
Melbourne, Australia, October 2023

Founder of PricingProphets.com | Author of:
"Overcoming Floccinaucinihilipilification: Valuing and Monetizing Products and Services"

CHAPTER 1

Navigating the Transformative Landscape of AI

1.1 INTRODUCTION

What comes to the average person's mind when asked about artificial intelligence (AI) data and advanced analytics? Most individuals' first thoughts would likely gravitate to the recent viral sensation, ChatGPT. While it is not the only impressive development in the industry, ChatGPT's virality has brought worldwide attention to the vast realm of AI and data.

Seasoned AI and analytics experts would contend that the AI language model ChatGPT represents merely a fraction of the immense potential that lies within the field. Even before ChatGPT, numerous other breakthroughs have transformed how we interact with technology. However, visionaries in the industry have demonstrated that ChatGPT's emergence is the transformative ripple that has significantly altered the landscape, further propelling the development and application of AI, data and analytics.

AI language models have made great strides in recent years. Nonetheless, ChatGPT's unparalleled ability to comprehend and generate texts that personify natural human speech has the global population imagining and exploring endless possibilities that are no longer distant achievements or fables of fiction. It has pushed boundaries, reshaping our perception of progress within the field of AI.

DOI: 10.1201/9781003408222-1

As we venture into this new era, reflecting on the history of AI, data and analytics is crucial. The evolution of AI began with simple algorithms and rule-based systems. Now, it learns patterns and makes predictions based on examples. Modern advanced analytics tools, developed through refined machine learning techniques, allow us to process vast amounts of data and generate valuable insights. These advancements have fuelled the growth of many industries and will continue to fuel the growth trajectories of many more. Its implications and benefits are vast, from finance and healthcare to entertainment and education.

As impressive as the journey has been thus far, we must acknowledge that there are challenges ahead. In the marketplace, popularity begets demand, and demand begets imitation. As organisations compete to satisfy the growing demand, they must confront issues arising from the increasing integration of AI, data and analytics in our lives. This pervasive influence necessitates addressing critical issues such as data privacy, algorithmic bias and the ethical implications of AI-driven decision-making. Additionally, organisations must effectively harness the power of advanced analytics to drive tangible value and secure a return on their analytics investments.

"Transition to Advanced Analytics: Get a Return on Your Analytics Investment" is your comprehensive guide to navigating and leveraging the complex landscape of AI, data and analytics.

It will shed light on both history and future insights, and it will also delve into revolutionary breakthroughs like ChatGPT. By the end of this book, you will be equipped to anticipate challenges and seize opportunities that await you in this exciting new era. Through the acquired knowledge that empowers you to uphold the balance between technological progress and ethical considerations, you will help welcome a future that benefits us all.

1.2 A GLIMPSE OF THE FUTURE: CONVERSATIONAL AI TECHNOLOGIES

User: "<AI NAME>, please search and purchase the latest Apple product for me."

AI Companion: "I've searched the nearest grocer's website. There should be a new batch of apples that came in yesterday. How many would you like me to buy?"

User: "What? No! <AI NAME>, search for the latest product from the company Apple, and get that purchased for me."

AI Companion: "I know. I also know your bank account balance, <USER>... And I'm merely suggesting a debt-free alternative."

The concept of AI engaging in open-ended conversations and providing contextual responses in human-like language was once only conceivable in science fiction. After all, traditional approaches to software, AI, data and analytics relied on predefined workflows and rigid user interfaces. These approaches have limitations, namely the system's flexibility and adaptability. We would interact with technology through buttons, menus or specific input fields. These predefined, structured interaction options focus on particular tasks or functionalities, leading to limited responses.

As natural language processing capabilities continue to improve, we can expect a significant shift in how users interact with software and analytics platforms. ChatGPT lies at the core of groundbreaking technologies, not only capturing the imagination of technologies and researchers alike but also opening up and paving the way for endless possibilities in the field. Pioneers in the industry train AI models like ChatGPT on vast amounts of textual data, allowing them to integrate with other software and execute a wide array of tasks via natural language interactions.

The vector database technology, once only affordable to Big Tech like Google and Bing, is now readily available and accessible to everyone. It empowers AI systems, enabling efficient storage and retrieval of unstructured information for quick access and real-time data processing. The development of large language models, combined with the power of vector databases, has revolutionised how we approach natural language understanding and processing. It is also these advancements that are poised to reshape the way we design software and advanced analytics solutions.

In a similar vein to how the fictional character Iron Man could interact with his AI companion J.A.R.V.I.S., users will soon have the opportunity to indulge in more interactive experiences. Engaging with software and analytics systems would feel like interacting with another person. Through natural language, users can instruct systems to perform various actions without being confined to rigid workflows or interfaces.

As we move towards free-flowing, conversational interactivity with technology as seen in Figure 1.1, we can anticipate a multitude of advantages:

- **Natural and intuitive communication:** Users will no longer have to learn complex commands or navigate through menus. They can communicate freely, making it more intuitive and accessible to people of all backgrounds and skill levels.

A Glimpse of The Future: Conversational AI Technologies

FIGURE 1.1 A timeline showing how we have moved past rigid interfaces to receive output and are in the era of natural language interfaces.

- **Revolutionised user experience:** Users will enjoy the personalised experience as the software can adapt to specific needs and preferences and offer dynamic responses.

- **Increased efficiency and convenience:** The advancements in AI, data and analytics will allow quick and efficient access to information, services and tasks. Users can acquire instant responses to their questions, perform complex tasks, obtain actionable insights and improve decision-making without going through multiple steps or complicated interfaces.

- **Inclusivity:** Those who find the traditional approaches challenging, such as those with limited technological literacy, will benefit from these conversational technologies.

- **Contextual understanding:** Developing more powerful and intelligent systems will retain previous interactions and use that knowledge to provide more accurate and relevant responses, enhancing the quality of interactions and allowing for more coherent and meaningful conversations.

- **Continuous improvement:** The technologies will continue to refine their responses and expand their knowledge base by analysing user feedback and data over time.

These advanced systems will open up new opportunities for innovation and collaboration across various industries. As we look towards the future, it is clear that the marriage of large language models and vector databases will continue to push the boundaries of what is possible in AI, data and analytics. By embracing these technological advancements and fostering an environment of continuous learning and innovation, we can unlock the full potential of AI and ensure a brighter, more connected future.

1.3 GUARDRAILS: DATA GOVERNANCE, PRIVACY, ETHICAL AND RESPONSIBLE AI

While advanced technologies hold tremendous potential to transform how we live and work, they also present unique data governance and privacy challenges. The infamous Cambridge Analytica and Facebook scandal is a testament to how inappropriate data utilisation can harm society (Zialcita, 2019). Hence, analytics professionals, organisations and enthusiasts must be vigilant in addressing challenges arising from data abuse and misuse. Given their importance, we explore these topics in more detail in Chapter 5 – Ensuring Your Advanced Analytics House Has a Solid Foundation and Chapter 10 – Communication, Ethics and Corporate Governance.

Data Governance and Privacy Protection

Establishing robust data governance and privacy protection policies is vital to safeguard the general population from negative repercussions. They will serve as the foundation for organisations to produce revenue-optimised analytics programmes while protecting the interests of individuals, communities and society as a whole.

Data governance and privacy protection are essential in maintaining trust and fostering a responsible approach to using data. By implementing robust data governance frameworks, organisations can ensure that the data they collect, store and analyse is managed in accordance with relevant laws and regulations. This includes setting clear guidelines for data collection, storage and usage, as well as enforcing stringent security measures to prevent unauthorised access or breaches. By taking these steps, we can mitigate the risks associated with data misuse and protect the data privacy of individuals. We will explore data governance in more detail in Chapter 5 – Ensuring Your Advanced Analytics House Has a Solid Foundation.

Responsible and Ethical AI

Similarly, the responsible and ethical use of AI is crucial in guiding the development and deployment of advanced analytics and AI systems.

To create responsible AI solutions, we must consider the ethical implications of our algorithms. To navigate the complex landscape of AI responsibly, we must consider aspects such as potential biases, fairness and transparency. By infusing ethical considerations into every stage of the AI development process, we can ensure that our systems are designed with societal well-being in mind, minimising the potential for negative consequences or harm.

In conclusion, our responsibility as analytics professionals extends beyond generating revenue for our organisations. Our work must align with data governance, privacy as well as responsible and ethical AI principles. By upholding these values, we can contribute to a world where advanced analytics and AI are used to create positive change, protect individual rights and foster a more equitable, just and sustainable society. We will explore this important topic further in Chapter 10 – Communication, Ethics and Corporate Governance.

1.4 ORGANISATIONAL AND TECHNICAL CHALLENGES

Preparation mitigates risks and ensures successful business transitions.

The implementation of advanced analytics poses numerous organisational and technical challenges. Enterprises must consider factors that minimise the impact of advanced analytics on their businesses:

- **Lack of understanding:** Many enterprises possess a superficial understanding of how data and analytics technologies operate. Their knowledge is often limited to surface-level concepts, similar to having a general idea about how ChatGPT functions without truly grasping the intricacies that drive its capabilities.

- **Data silos:** When different departments within an organisation utilise separate systems and databases, it becomes challenging to integrate and analyse data effectively.

- **Limited resources:** Some enterprises may not have the ability to invest in the financial and human resources required to implement and maintain data analytics solutions.

- **Fear of change:** Implementing data analytics solutions may require significant changes to existing processes and workflows, which can be challenging and disruptive to some enterprises.

- **Data quality issues:** Some enterprises may not have the necessary resources or processes in place to ensure data quality. Thus, poor data quality will negatively impact the accuracy and effectiveness of advanced analytics.

- **Lack of clear goals and objectives:** Measuring success and achieving desired outcomes are problematic when data analytics initiatives lack clear goals and objectives.

- **Compatibility:** Cloud computing often clashes with legacy systems that some industries continue to rely on. These archaic systems date back to the 1980s, making it difficult for enterprises to enhance data and analytics capabilities for effective integration into their business operations.

- **Regulatory and compliance concerns:** Advanced analytics may require access to sensitive or personal data, which can raise concerns about compliance with regulatory requirements such as General Data Protection Regulation (GDPR), California Consumer Privacy Act (CCPA) and Australian Privacy Principles (APPs).

In addition to the challenges mentioned above, enterprises that are migrating their advanced analytics operations to the cloud computing environment will face additional obstacles, including the following:

- **New architecture:** The lift and shift approach that many organisations adopted to migrate their data analytics capabilities poses an ongoing issue (*Lift and Shift: An Essential Guide*, n.d.). Some have found it necessary to completely redesign their data warehouse architecture and business intelligence (BI) capabilities as they transitioned to cloud computing.

- **Data security:** Security becomes a major concern during the data migration process. Enterprises must ensure that their data is protected and that their cloud service providers implement appropriate security measures.

- **Skills and expertise:** The cloud computing environment requires specialised skills and expertise. Enterprises may need to train their staff or recruit new talent to oversee their data capabilities within the cloud infrastructure proficiently.

- **Governance and compliance:** Enterprises must also comply with relevant regulations and governance policies when migrating data to the cloud. These policies include data privacy, data residency and data retention.

Addressing these challenges and investing in the necessary resources and expertise can help organisations realise the full potential of advanced analytics and drive business growth. In subsequent chapters, we will provide technical and organisational implementation frameworks. Alongside these frameworks, we will share practical insights that will help you get a head start on implementation and yield substantial returns for your investment. These are explored further in Chapters 5–9 and an approach is shared that can help you navigate these challenges.

CHAPTER 2

Adapting to Technological Shifts

The Evolution of Software, Data, Analytics and AI

2.1 THE EVOLUTION OF SOFTWARE, DATA, ANALYTICS AND AI

Data and analytics preceded ChatGPT and have been around for centuries. However, it was in the Information Age that D+A became intrinsic to modern life.

In the early stages, data analysis heavily relied on manual methods such as paper-based calculations and categorisation. During this time, the impact of data remained restricted due to the limited availability of technology during that period.

Late 1800s to Mid 1900s

Businesses widely used technologies such as punch cards, analogue computers and electromechanical calculators (*Analog Computer*, n.d.; Maxfield, 2005; *The IBM Punched Card*, n.d.). These technologies helped store and process data more efficiently. Subsequently, they played a pivotal role in guiding companies' production, marketing and customer satisfaction decisions, empowering them to make informed choices.

DOI: 10.1201/9781003408222-2

1970s

The development of microprocessors marked a turning point in data research. Computers enable businesses to analyse information quickly and accurately. By this time, databases could store large volumes of data in a structured format.

Users also saw an influx of more sophisticated analytical software programs in the 1970s. Software packages like Statistical Package for the Social Sciences (SPSS) and Statistical Analysis System (SAS) were developed for statistical and data analysis. Even without extensive programming knowledge, users could run statistical models.

1980s

Users during this time saw breakthroughs in digital technology. There was greater access to powerful computing resources, with reliable personal storage devices paving the way for big data storage solutions for enterprise businesses (*Memory & Storage,* n.d.). Companies could accumulate massive amounts of customer information, leading to a surge in sophisticated analytics capabilities across industries like banking and retailing.

1990s

The digital storage landscape witnessed the emergence of Storage Area Networks (SAN) and Network-Attached Storage Arrays (NAS) in the years leading up to the 2000s. As maintenance and upgrade costs skyrocketed due to growing file sizes and volumes, the development of more efficient and innovative solutions came as a reprieve to enterprises (*The Evolution of Enterprise Data Storage,* 2020).

With the massive growth in Internet adoption in the late 1990s, the use of application systems grew exponentially. By 2000, enterprises were bombarded with new technological issues that came with large data storage capacities and application systems. They were bombarded with large volumes of fragmented data, and their systems were so poorly integrated that they led to data inconsistency (Foote, 2023).

While the concept of data warehousing has circulated since the 1980s, it was during the dot.com bubble era that enterprises truly saw the need for data integration (*Data Warehouse,* 2021). The introduction of data warehouses gave rise to management information systems (MIS). Organisations of all sizes, from large enterprises to small startups, could use business intelligence (BI) tools. Albeit lacking in present-day capabilities such as predictive analytics, complex algorithms and machine learning (ML), they laid down the foundations that would power what we know as modern analytics today.

2000s

From the early 2000s, the role of BI and MIS in organisations has only grown in importance. Companies now rely on MIS to collect, store and analyse data from diverse sources, enabling them to uncover valuable insights that impact their operations and make better-informed decisions. Additionally, MIS allows monitoring performance metrics in near real-time, providing the agility to adapt and adjust when required.

BI tools have integrated seamlessly into modern MIS solutions, providing executives and decision-makers access to updated information on key metrics and performance indicators at any time. These insights facilitate efficient decision-making, enabling teams to identify improvement areas and offer competitive advantages over their industry counterparts.

In short, advanced analytics made significant strides during this decade, marked by key developments such as the widespread adoption of data warehousing, BI and MIS.

2010 and Beyond

Cloud computing has been experiencing a growing surge in popularity within the business sphere since the 2010s. Large enterprises are migrating their systems, data, analytics and technology stacks to the cloud. The rising popularity and user-friendly nature of cloud computing signify yet another transformative shift in the realm of data and analytics.

Due to its scalable and flexible infrastructure, it accelerated the development of technologies that demand massive computing power. With these vast computing resources, Big Tech companies could leverage, explore and deploy sophisticated artificial intelligence (AI) and ML algorithms for various application systems. These AI models subsequently enable companies to make breakthroughs in computer vision, natural language processing (NLP) and other related fields.

As researchers and engineers diligently improved the models to interpret and grasp visual or textual data, they opened up exciting possibilities like intelligent AI assistants and sentiment analysis. The massive successes of those huge companies fuelled greater awareness of AI and ML's potential across industries. Recognising the competitive advantages of advanced analytics, businesses in the Fortune 500 quickly took notice and invested heavily in these transformative technologies (*KPMG Report*, 2019).

2.2 THE SHIFT IN FOCUS

From the technology evolution timeline, it becomes evident that organisations initially prioritised process digitisation and consolidating data into centralised systems. Enterprise software served as a means to streamline operations and enhance efficiency, enabling companies to manage their resources better and improve overall performance. These systems laid the groundwork for a new era of data-driven decision-making, as they allowed organisations to collect, store and analyse vast volumes of information.

In recent decades, industries and companies worldwide have embraced the transformative potential of software and BI. This shift has led to a significant increase in investment and procurement of enterprise systems and BI tools, underscoring the growing recognition of the value of data-driven decision-making and the necessity for agile, scalable technology solutions.

As BI tools progressed, they offered increasingly sophisticated analytics capabilities. Companies could now access and analyse their data in near real-time, enabling them to discern trends, uncover hidden patterns and make well-informed decisions. This data-driven approach to decision-making has since become a cornerstone of contemporary business strategy, with companies from diverse sectors harnessing BI to gain a competitive edge.

Today, we stand at the forefront of yet another momentous shift. Advancements in AI, data and analytics are pushing the boundaries of what we can achieve with technology. We are augmenting traditional BI tools. Other times, we are replacing them with advanced analytics solutions with ML and AI capabilities. These systems not only allow for more complex analysis but also offer predictive and prescriptive insights, empowering companies to anticipate future trends, optimise their operations and drive innovation.

In the coming years, the integration of AI, data and analytics will continue to revolutionise industries and redefine how companies operate. We expect to see even more sophisticated AI-driven analytics solutions that can process and analyse data at unprecedented speeds and scale. These tools will enable companies to gain deeper insights into their operations, customers and markets, allowing for more precise and targeted decision-making.

Furthermore, as discussed earlier, the advancement of NLP capabilities will likely reshape how users interact with software and analytics platforms. Organisations that embrace these technologies and invest in their development will be well-positioned to capitalise on the wealth of opportunities.

To conclude, the past, current and future of data, analytics and AI are inextricably linked, with each stage building upon the successes and learnings of its predecessors. As we continue to innovate and explore new frontiers in AI, data and analytics, we must also remember the importance of data governance, privacy, and responsible and ethical AI. By doing so, we ensure that the growth and adoption of these technologies lead to positive outcomes for organisations and society at large.

2.3 THE GREAT DIVERGENCE

In today's rapidly evolving business landscape, we see the coexistence of two distinct types of companies as depicted in Figure 2.1 below. Each category approaches software, data and AI differently, reflecting their unique priorities, goals and strategies. We will examine their approaches and strategies, exploring the strengths and weaknesses of each type of company.

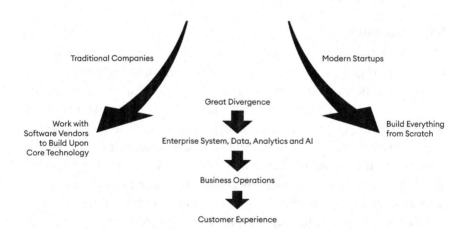

FIGURE 2.1   A diagram depicting the distinctive approaches to software, data and AI taken by traditional companies and modern startups, respectively. Traditional companies work with software vendors to build upon their core technology, whereas modern startups build everything from the ground up.

This in-depth understanding will allow you to make strategic decisions investing in advanced analytics for enterprises and government agencies.

Traditional Companies

Traditional companies have long-established roots in their respective industries. These organisations focus on delivering exceptional customer service and maintaining their core business operations. To accomplish these goals, they often acquire enterprise software and data analytics solutions from software vendors. These solutions aid in streamlining processes, managing resources and making informed decisions.

An example of this category is the traditional banking sector, which has existed for decades, if not centuries. Companies such as JPMorgan Chase & Co., Bank of America and Wells Fargo have built their businesses on trust and reliability, providing essential financial services to customers worldwide.

To support their operations, these banks invest in a range of core enterprise software and data analytics solutions. These range from customer intelligence, voice of customer, risk management, compliance solutions, fraud analytics and more.

By leveraging these technologies, traditional banks can enhance their decision-making capabilities, optimise their operations and cater to the needs of their customers more effectively.

Modern Startups

Modern startups adopt an innovative approach within their chosen industries. These organisations prioritise the development of their unique core software solutions, often combining cutting-edge data, analytics and AI capabilities to deliver exceptional customer experience. By building custom software and integrating advanced analytics, these companies can differentiate themselves from competitors and disrupt traditional industry norms.

A prime illustration of this category is the search engine industry, which has transformed through the emergence of companies like Google. Through developing proprietary algorithms and harnessing the potential of data and AI, Google has revolutionised how people discover and access information online.

Another noteworthy example is the online streaming sector. Within this industry, companies like Netflix and Spotify have leveraged data analytics and AI to provide personalised recommendations and curated content for their users (O'Reilly, 2016; Sletten, 2021).

Similarly, social networking platforms like Facebook and Twitter have built their businesses around analysing and understanding user data. They employ AI-driven insights to create engaging and relevant experiences for their users (e.g., Tønnesen and Tennfjord, 2023).

Coexistence between Traditional Companies and Modern Startups

The coexistence of these two company types highlights the diverse approaches to software, data and AI in today's business landscape. Each category possesses its own strengths, challenges and unique opportunities for growth and innovation.

Traditional companies, bolstered by their loyal customer bases and extensive industry expertise, can leverage technology to enhance their existing operations and swiftly adapt to evolving market dynamics. Conversely, startups that centre their businesses around advanced software, data and AI capabilities hold the potential to disrupt industries and redefine how customers interact with products and services.

2.4 CHALLENGES AND CONSTRAINTS IN SOFTWARE AND DATA APPROACHES FOR BUSINESS OPERATIONS

As a result of their distinct approaches to software, data and analytics, both traditional companies and modern startups will encounter unique constraints and challenges in the years ahead. Each type of organisation must navigate these complexities to remain competitive and relevant in an increasingly data-driven business landscape.

Traditional Companies

While traditional companies benefit from well-established customer bases, industry expertise, stability and a deep understanding of their markets, they must also contend with numerous challenges.

Their reliance on legacy systems, the difficulty of integrating modern advanced analytics and AI solutions and the resulting complexity and inefficiency present significant obstacles. We will explore these challenges and constraints in more detail through the following sections.

Reliance on Legacy Systems

Traditional companies encounter a significant challenge due to their reliance on enterprise software developed decades ago. These legacy systems could date back 20 years ago or more (Sudarsan, Mohan and Rohit, 2018). While crucial to past success, they are challenging to modify and integrate with modern advanced analytics and AI products. The original architecture of these systems lacks the flexibility and scalability required in today's rapidly evolving technology landscape. As a result, traditional companies face obstacles in their progress and competitiveness within the market.

Additional Workflow and Software Application

To overcome the limitations of their core enterprise systems, many traditional companies resort to implementing additional workflows and software applications. In their efforts to bridge the wide gap between legacy systems and desired advanced analytics solutions, frontline employees must navigate numerous software applications while adhering to detailed manual instructions to serve their clients effectively.

Impact on User Experience and Productivity

A fragmented and disjointed user experience for employees naturally follows after various applications and workflows are introduced. The complex workflows and multiple applications may negatively impact their productivity. Furthermore, they could result in errors and delays when servicing clients. Over time, these inefficiencies compound, making it even more challenging for traditional companies to successfully integrate new analytics solutions into their existing technology stacks.

Meeting the Demands of a Changing Landscape

As demand for advanced analytics solutions grows, traditional companies struggle to keep pace with innovation and meet client demands. The longer these organisations delay modernising their technology infrastructure and adopting advanced analytics and AI solutions, the more arduous it becomes to remain competitive in an increasingly data-driven world.

Change Resistance

Traditional companies must be prepared to face resistance from employees and stakeholders. Established processes and workflows, ingrained culture and hierarchical systems within these organisations are natural and anticipated barriers to adopting new technologies and practices. Employees and stakeholders may resist changes that disrupt established routines and familiar standard operating procedures (SOPs). They may also be reluctant to acquire new knowledge and skills. Consequently, change resistance can impede the company's progress in modernising its technology infrastructure and hinder the adoption of advanced analytics and AI solutions. In Chapters 5–9, we will look at ways this resistance can be overcome in a traditional company. In particular, in Chapter 9, we will explore the importance of an agile mindset and approach.

Modern Startups

Conversely, modern startups often begin with a clean slate, unburdened by legacy systems and processes. This allows them to build their businesses around the latest technology, seamlessly integrating advanced data, analytics and AI capabilities from the outset. Consequently, they can establish highly efficient and agile operations that can readily adapt to changes in the market.

However, startups also encounter their own set of challenges, including the need to establish credibility, build a customer base and secure funding to support their growth. Additionally, they may face regulatory hurdles as they disrupt traditional industries and introduce new business models.

As the business landscape continues to evolve, organisations of all types need to adapt and embrace the transformative power of technology. By doing so, they can remain competitive, drive growth and shape the future of their industries. Regardless of the type of company, it is crucial to acknowledge the value of software, data and analytics and their contributions to shaping their futures.

By embracing these technologies and incorporating them into their business strategies, companies can unlock new avenues for growth, enhance operational efficiency and customer satisfaction. For traditional companies, this may mean investing in modernising their systems and fostering a culture of innovation. For startups, this may involve establishing trust and credibility while continuously refining their offerings based on customer needs and feedback.

2.5 UNFAIR ADVANTAGES OF MODERN STARTUPS

Modern startups stand out from traditional companies by making a deliberate choice to construct their core enterprise systems from scratch. This strategic decision grants them greater control and flexibility in designing and modifying their business software. By having complete autonomy in system development, startups gain a unique advantage that can translate into significant competitive advantages.

One such advantage is their enhanced data collection and insights. Startups have a greater ability to collect extensive data about customers, products and services. Their systems are designed with modern data collection and storage practices in mind, allowing them to capture a wealth of information effortlessly. This comprehensive and detailed data serves as a strong foundation for startups to gain deeper customer insights and refine their offerings, driving innovation and fostering growth.

Additionally, modern startups can develop and embed advanced analytics solutions directly into their software and existing workflows. This integration enables them to incorporate data-driven insights and recommendations into their operations, facilitating more informed decision-making, process optimisation and improved customer experiences. This stands in contrast to traditional companies, which often struggle to integrate advanced analytics solutions into their legacy systems and workflows.

Modern startups are also better positioned to adapt to the rapidly evolving digital landscape. As their core systems are built from scratch around the latest technology, these companies are more agile and can readily embrace new trends and innovations as they emerge. This adaptability allows startups to stay ahead of the curve and continuously respond to digital adoption, maintaining their relevance and competitiveness in the market.

The advantages of modern startups extend to their frontline employees, who naturally benefit from streamlined workflows designed to incorporate data and advanced analytics solutions. These streamlined processes enable frontline employees to serve customers more efficiently. As a result, startups can deliver exceptional experiences to their clients, increasing customer satisfaction and loyalty.

Modern startups possess a myriad of advantages over traditional companies in the realms of software, data and analytics. Their ability to build and modify core enterprise systems from scratch, coupled with enhanced data collection, seamless integration of advanced analytics and agile adaptability to digital trends, positions them for success in the competitive business landscape.

2.6 GENERATIVE AI's RAPID ADVANCEMENTS: DISRUPTIVE OR TRANSFORMATIONAL?

The rapid advancements in generative AI and large language models are driving a new wave of technological innovation with the potential to disrupt startups established over the last 20 years. This transformation is reshaping how we interact with software and serve customers, affecting both traditional companies and existing modern startups.

Presently, software and enterprise systems utilised by traditional companies and modern startups rely on pre-configured workflows to achieve the desired results. These workflows, designed by user experience designers and programmers, dictate the flow of business activities for customers and employees. As a result, users and employees must adhere to the prescribed instructions to accomplish their objectives.

However, the emergence of large language models such as GPT-4 is set to revolutionise user interactions with products and businesses, as well as how employees serve customers using software. These AI-driven systems have the potential to transform user interactions, enabling more natural, intuitive and contextually aware communication and problem-solving. This paradigm shift promotes fluid and dynamic interactions, departing from our current reliance on fixed workflows.

The disruption could hold profound implications for both traditional companies and existing startups. The transformative power of large language models challenges these organisations' previous successes and fortunes as this wave of technological advancements gives rise to a new breed of startups. The new type of startups design software that seamlessly integrates data, analytics and advanced analytics with large language models, serving customers more effectively and efficiently.

Following current trends, these new startups may harness the power of generative AI to create software systems that intelligently adapt to user needs, offering personalised solutions and support without the limitations of pre-configured workflows. This dramatic shift in the competitive landscape will see these innovative newcomers challenging established incumbents with their agile and responsive solutions.

The impact of large language models extends to how employees use software to serve customers. With AI-driven systems understanding and responding to natural language, employees can quickly access information, resolve issues and collaborate more effectively without rigid workflows. This increased efficiency, productivity and customer satisfaction will transcend multiple industries.

As history repeats itself, we witness the potential reversal of roles. Startups that once disrupted traditional companies may face disruption by more innovative newcomers. Armed with generative AI and large language models, these emerging players are poised to redefine the landscape

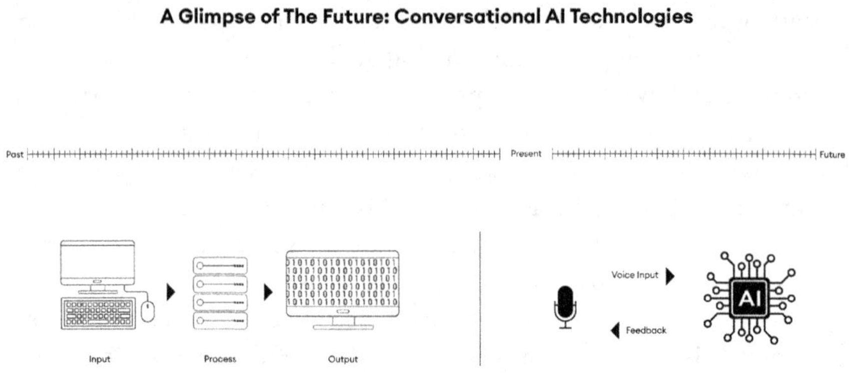

A Glimpse of The Future: Conversational AI Technologies

FIGURE 2.2   A timeline showing how we have moved past rigid interfaces to receive output and are in the era of natural language interfaces.

of software design and usage, forever altering the fields of customer service and business operations. Recognizing and adapting to these changes in technology, as mapped in Figure 2.2, will position companies better for success in this rapidly evolving environment. It is an exciting and unpredictable time as we stand on the precipice of a new era in technology that could redefine how we live and work.

CHAPTER 3

Future-Proofing Organisations with Embedded Advanced Analytics

We have observed the divergence between traditional companies and modern startups in their approach to using software to run their businesses, a trend that will undoubtedly continue. Nevertheless, it is crucial to acknowledge that there is no one-size-fits-all solution to software and data utilisation. After all, each company has its own unique strengths, weaknesses and organisational structure. Understanding all these aspects will determine the best course of action.

3.1 MACRO DIRECTIONS FOR TRADITIONAL COMPANIES

Let us revisit key points on traditional companies.

- They have cultivated a decades-long understanding of their customers and industries.

- They possess a wealth of experience that serves as a strong foundation for success in the digital age.

DOI: 10.1201/9781003408222-3

Instead of developing their own core enterprise software, traditional companies can explore partnerships with software vendors that specialise in building modern, digital-first solutions tailored to their specific industry needs. It would save them from venturing into a path that may prove less effective or efficient.

It is worth noting that new software vendors are developing next-generation enterprise software specifically for traditional companies. In fact, there is a growing ecosystem of software vendors dedicated to creating cloud-native, data-driven software solutions for traditional businesses. These vendors understand these entities' challenges and opportunities and are committed to bridging the gap between these organisations and their more technologically advanced counterparts.

Traditional companies enjoy numerous benefits by embracing the software vendors' modern software solutions.

Modern software solutions allow traditional companies to focus on their core competencies – customer service, product development and market expansion. These companies can leverage characteristics of cloud-native applications, known for their agility, adaptability and data-driven nature.

These applications, built specifically for the cloud, take advantage of cloud computing's scalability, flexibility and cost efficiency. As a result of leveraging the latest innovations and best practices in their industry, traditional companies can stay ahead of the curve and easily adapt to the changing needs and demands of traditional companies, enabling them to remain competitive in an increasingly digital landscape.

Cloud-native applications often feature open architectures and APIs, enabling easy connectivity with other software solutions and seamless data sharing (Abernathey et al., 2021). This facilitates the creation of an integrated software ecosystem that supports a wide range of business processes and functions. Consequently, traditional companies can break free from the constraints of legacy systems and siloed data, streamlining their operations and improving overall efficiency.

By providing secure and efficient mechanisms for sharing data between applications, these cloud-native platforms also enable traditional companies to unlock the full potential of their data assets. This leads to more informed decision-making, enhanced collaboration and, ultimately, better business outcomes.

On top of data sharing and integration capabilities, the cloud-native architecture of modern software applications allows for regular updates and enhancements, ensuring they remain up to date with the latest technological advancements and industry best practices. This empowers traditional companies to keep pace with the rapidly evolving digital landscape and maintain a competitive edge in their respective markets.

With the power of data and advanced analytics, modern software applications provide actionable insights and recommendations to support better decision-making at all organisational levels. This empowers traditional companies to leverage data as a strategic asset, unlocking new opportunities for growth and innovation.

In brief, it is crucial to recognise that no universal strategy for success exists. Traditional companies can continue leveraging their strengths, focusing on their deep industry knowledge and customer insights while embracing modern, digital-first solutions tailored to their unique needs. By adopting this balanced approach, traditional organisations can maintain their competitive advantage and thrive in an increasingly digital world.

3.2 ADVANCED ANALYTICS AND GENERATIVE AI TO FUTURE-PROOF TRADITIONAL COMPANIES

Nevertheless, traditional companies should not become complacent with specialised software vendors in the face of rapid technological advancements. Instead, they must actively invest in their own data, analytics and artificial intelligence (AI) technology stacks, ensuring that their systems and processes are effective not just for today but also ready to adapt to the evolving landscape of the future.

Traditional companies must consider how their existing data, analytics and AI solutions will integrate with new systems as they plan to replace or modernise their legacy enterprise software. This involves evaluating compatibility with emerging software offerings, scalability and the ability to adapt to changing business needs and customer expectations.

To future-proof their analytics and AI capabilities, traditional companies should seek vendors offering open, modular architectures. These architectures allow for seamless integration with existing technology stacks and the incorporation of new tools and technologies. Additionally, solutions support a wide range of integrations with other software and their data. Such solutions ensure that their analytics and AI systems can accommodate the growing diversity and complexity of data generated by modern businesses.

Traditional companies must also encourage the adoption of a change mindset, foster experimentation and empower employees to explore new ideas and technologies. By instilling this culture throughout the organisation, traditional companies can capitalise on advancements in data, analytics and AI while adapting to the ever-shifting digital landscape. We explore this in more detail and propose an approach to achieve this in Chapters 5–9.

Moreover, a proactive approach to developing data, analytics and AI technology stacks can lead to substantial cost savings and increased operational efficiency. Subsequently, organisations can adapt to new challenges and opportunities without major overhauls or system replacements.

Legacy systems will eventually become obsolete. As such, traditional companies should avoid costly mistakes and extensive, large-scale projects in the future through careful planning and foresight. Integrating analytics and AI solutions with new software systems from the outset ensures a seamless transition process, minimising disruptions and effectively leveraging valuable data and insights.

A well-thought-out strategy for integrating data, analytics and AI technologies with new enterprise software helps traditional companies maintain a competitive edge in the marketplace. Leveraging an API framework to share and ingest data enables this approach, allowing companies to stay ahead.

3.3 ADVANTAGES OF STRATEGIC AND GRADUAL MIGRATIONS FOR TRADITIONAL COMPANIES

As mentioned previously, traditional companies must anticipate the replacement of enterprise software and carefully plan the integration of their data, analytics and AI technologies with new enterprise software. Making early preparations will provide these companies with various key advantages.

With careful planning, companies can avoid running large, simultaneous replacement programmes. This can be highly beneficial for traditional companies, as it enables them to spread their investments and resources over time, mitigating the risks and disruptions associated with large-scale overhauls.

Simultaneous revamps of an organisation's analytics infrastructure may cause significant disruptions to its daily operations. A staggered approach helps maintain business continuity and prevents operational bottlenecks that may arise from implementing multiple complex system replacements simultaneously (Giles, 2008).

Decoupling the replacement of enterprise software from the analytics solution enables traditional companies to prioritise areas that offer the greatest potential for business impact and return on investment (ROI) while ensuring the effective functioning of critical systems and processes.

The staggered approach to system replacement provides employees with time to build expertise and proficiency in new systems and processes. This leads to increased efficiency and productivity in the long run.

In summary, strategic planning and proactive management of the integration between enterprise software and data, analytics, and AI technologies offer substantial benefits for traditional companies. By ensuring adaptability and future readiness, these organisations can prolong the ROI of their current solutions, reduce the risk of costly mistakes and large-scale projects and maintain a competitive advantage in an increasingly data-driven business environment.

3.4 THE RIGHT TERMINOLOGIES: ADVANCED ANALYTICS VERSUS DATA ANALYTICS AND BUSINESS INTELLIGENCE

Before we delve into the second part of our exploration into advanced analytics, let us first establish a clear distinction between advanced analytics and data analytics. Despite the growing significance of these terms in the business world, professionals remain confused about their differences and how they are applied in practice.

Data analytics and business intelligence are crucial in providing insights into an organisation's past performance and current state. They help companies understand their business performance in-depth using techniques such as data visualisation, reporting and basic statistical analysis. However, these methods often fall short when anticipating future events or suggesting optimal courses of action. This is where advanced analytics comes in, offering a more comprehensive approach to data-driven decision-making.

Advanced analytics leverages sophisticated techniques and tools such as machine learning, artificial intelligence (AI) and natural language processing (NLP) to uncover hidden patterns and relationships in data. It enables organisations to understand past events, predict future outcomes and make better-informed decisions. In other words, advanced analytics diverges from data analytics and business intelligence in terms of approach. In Figure 3.1, we make a comparison between the data analytics approach and the advanced analytics approach. While data analytics and business intelligence primarily focus on historical trends and descriptive analysis, advanced analytics is one step ahead by employing predictive and prescriptive analysis.

Data Analytics vs Advanced Analytics

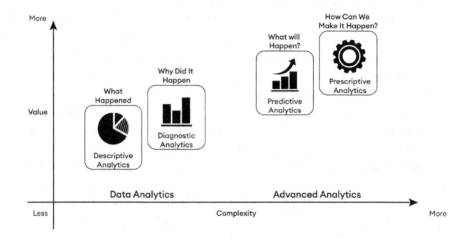

FIGURE 3.1 A chart demonstrating the differences between data analytics and advanced analytics, with advanced analytics being more complex by nature but providing higher value. Descriptive analytics (what happened) and diagnostic analytics (why did it happen) are the two types of data analytics. Predictive analytics (what will happen) and prescriptive analytics (how can we make it happen) fall under advanced analytics.

Techniques Used in Advanced Analytics

Advanced analytics is an umbrella term for a suite of techniques and capabilities organisations leverage to gain a deeper understanding of their data and extract valuable insights. It is these techniques that allow businesses to anticipate future trends, identify opportunities and make informed decisions. Let us delve into its various components and capabilities.

Predictive Modelling

Predictive modelling is a core technique utilising historical data and statistical algorithms to predict future events, trends or behaviours. It allows organisations to identify potential risks, uncover new opportunities and optimise strategies based on data-driven predictions. Common techniques in predictive modelling include regression analysis, time series analysis and machine learning algorithms such as decision trees, neural networks and ensemble methods.

Machine Learning

Machine learning is another vital aspect of advanced analytics. It falls within the subset of AI that involves developing algorithms that can learn and improve from experience without explicit programming.

Machine learning enables computers to recognise patterns, make decisions and adapt to new information autonomously. Techniques in machine learning can be broadly categorised as supervised learning, unsupervised learning and reinforcement learning.

- **Supervised learning** involves training a model using labelled data to make predictions and classify new, unseen data.

- **Unsupervised learning** deals with unlabelled data and relies on the algorithm to discover patterns and relationships.

- **Reinforcement learning** involves the AI model learning through interactions with its environment, guided by rewards or penalties.

Natural Language Processing (NLP)

As another crucial component of advanced analytics, NLP is the intersection of AI, computational linguistics and computer science. It enables computers to understand, interpret and generate human language. Additionally, NLP allows organisations to process large volumes of unstructured text data, such as customer reviews, social media posts and emails, to extract meaningful insights. NLP techniques include sentiment analysis, topic modelling, entity recognition and machine translation.

Optimisation and Simulation

Optimisation and simulation are also essential techniques in advanced analytics. Optimisation involves finding the best possible solution to a problem while considering constraints and objectives. It is widely used in areas such as supply chain management, scheduling and resource allocation.

On the other hand, simulation involves creating virtual models of systems or processes to study their behaviour and performance under various conditions (*Prescriptive Analytics*, 2020). By experimenting with different scenarios in simulated environments, organisations can gain insights into potential outcomes and identify optimal strategies.

Text Mining

Text mining focuses on extracting valuable information from large volumes of unstructured text data. It involves processing and analysing text data to identify patterns, trends and relationships that provide valuable insights for decision-making. An example of text mining applications includes sentiment analysis, which determines the sentiment or emotion expressed in text. Yet another example is document clustering, which groups documents based on their content similarity.

As seen in Figure 3.2, there are many other techniques in advanced analytics. However, they all share one objective: to anticipate future trends, identify opportunities and make informed decisions. Now that we have differentiated between the terminologies and delved into the intricacies of

Different Techniques in Advanced Analytics

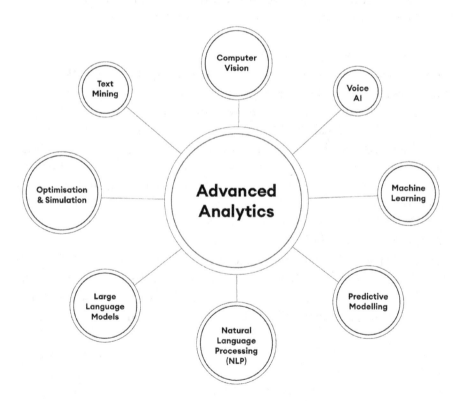

FIGURE 3.2 Different techniques in advanced analytics: Computer vision, voice AI, machine learning, predictive modelling, NLP, large language models, optimisation and simulation, and text mining.

advanced analytics, it may seem evident that advanced analytics and data analytics are two separate disciplines. However, several factors understandably contribute to the persistent confusion surrounding these terms.

Both advanced analytics and data analytics aim to generate insights from data and drive better decision-making within organisations. Furthermore, advanced analytics often builds upon the foundation laid by data analytics and business intelligence, incorporating their outputs into more complex models and analyses. As a result, professionals may struggle to discern the boundaries between these disciplines.

The Evolving Landscape of Data and Analytics

As new technologies emerge and existing techniques become more sophisticated, the line between data analytics and advanced analytics constantly shifts. For example, basic machine learning algorithms and similar tools that were once considered advanced are now becoming more commonplace in data analytics. This constant evolution makes it challenging for professionals to stay abreast with the latest developments and clearly understand the distinctions between these disciplines.

In essence, the critical difference between advanced analytics and data analytics lies in their approaches and depth of analysis. Advanced analytics employs more sophisticated techniques and tools to extract deeper insights from data, allowing organisations to predict future events and make prescriptive recommendations. In contrast, data analytics and business intelligence focus on understanding historical trends and providing descriptive analysis. Understanding this distinction is vital for organisations transitioning to advanced analytics and aiming to maximise their return on analytics investment.

In the following sections, we will delve further into the benefits of advanced analytics, the reasons organisations choose to embed it within their operations and real-world use cases that demonstrate its potential.

3.5 BENEFITS OF EMBRACING ADVANCED ANALYTICS

The value of advanced analytics is increasingly recognised by organisations across various industries, prompting them to actively incorporate it into their operations. We will explore in detail how embracing advanced analytics offers numerous benefits to organisations below.

Previously, we have explored how traditional companies can benefit from employing advanced analytics to guide their decisions and resource allocation. Veritably, all organisations stand to benefit in the same way.

Relying on intuition or anecdotal evidence pales in comparison to robust, evidence-based data that advanced analytics provides. By utilising advanced analytics to uncover hidden patterns and relationships in data, companies can identify trends, anticipate customer needs and adapt to changing market dynamics more effectively than their competitors.

By analysing large volumes of data, organisations can identify market gaps, emerging trends or unaddressed customer pain points. Armed with these insights, companies can create innovative products, services or business models that cater to these unmet needs, gaining a competitive edge and capturing new markets. Moreover, advanced analytics facilitates continuous improvement by enabling organisations to monitor the real-time performance of their offerings and make data-driven adjustments to optimise them.

Advanced analytics can streamline processes, reduce waste and increase productivity. Techniques such as optimisation and simulation allow organisations to optimise supply chain operations, identify bottlenecks and minimise costs using data-driven insights. Automating repetitive tasks through advanced analytics also frees employees to focus on higher-value activities, contributing to the overall growth and success of the company.

By leveraging techniques like NLP and machine learning, organisations can better understand customer preferences, sentiments and behaviour. With these insights, companies can create personalised experiences, tailor marketing campaigns and proactively address customer concerns. Ultimately, meeting and exceeding customer expectations foster loyalty, increase repeat business and improve the bottom line.

Finally, advanced analytics supports organisations by predicting potential risks, evaluating the impact of various scenarios and developing mitigation strategies and contingency plans. It aids in minimising disruptions, protecting assets and navigating regulatory and compliance challenges by monitoring and analysing relevant data to ensure adherence to industry standards and legal requirements.

In conclusion, companies can navigate the complexities of the modern business landscape, stay ahead of the competition and achieve sustained growth and success by embracing advanced analytics.

3.6 PUSHING THE BOUNDARIES WITH EMBEDDED ADVANCED ANALYTICS

Embedding advanced analytics is the next step after advanced analytics and goes beyond mere implementation within an organisation. The notion of "embedding" signifies the integration of advanced analytics with the organisation's infrastructure rather than a standalone component. This means that advanced analytics capabilities are interwoven with enterprise systems, customer touchpoints and employee workflows, thus breaking down data silos and creating a unified source of truth.

With data-driven insights that are accessible and actionable across all levels and functions, companies that ascribe to this data-driven culture will achieve a more cohesive and holistic approach to decision-making as well as drive innovation and growth. Organisations can streamline operations, reduce inefficiencies and ensure informed decision-making at the individual level by infusing advanced analytics capabilities into their employees' daily work tasks and processes.

Incorporating advanced analytics into customer-facing processes and applications allows organisations to better understand customer needs, preferences and behaviour. Through these insights, organisations can create personalised, enjoyable customer experiences and foster loyalty. Moreover, embedded advanced analytics can help them proactively identify customer pain points, predict churn and address concerns before they escalate, leading to enhanced customer satisfaction and retention.

In short, embedded advanced analytics emphasises the importance of making advanced analytics an integral part of the organisation's DNA, ensuring that its benefits permeate all aspects of one's business. An example of how advanced analytics and embedded advanced can analytics optimise business operations is shown in Figure 3.3.

Advanced analytics and embedded advanced analytics solutions do not only retail businesses. In Figure 3.4, it is evident that such solutions also prove effective in optimising prices for insurance companies.

By comparing the two diagrams above, it is evident that advanced analytics and embedded advanced analytics can be used to solve dynamic pricing challenges across multiple sectors.

While using the same techniques to optimise pricing, retailers and insurers alike can benefit from embedding advanced analytics into their daily operations. Embedding advanced analytics allows retailers to eliminate manual updates and the use of multiple interfaces in tandem. On the other hand, it allows insurers to eliminate cognitive loading and tough decision-making for sales teams in call centres.

Beyond retail and insurance, many software and technology in the current market also leverage embedded advanced analytics to reduce friction in the user workflow. An example is Engage AI. As shown in Figure 3.5, the technology is able to streamline its users' workflow on LinkedIn.

Advanced Analytics vs Embedded Advanced Analytics for Product Pricing in Retail

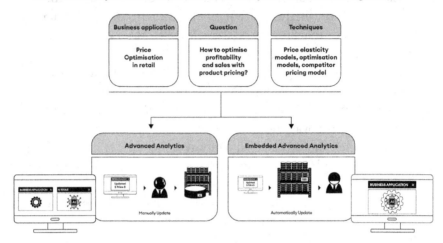

FIGURE 3.3 Hierarchical diagram showing advanced analytics and embedded advanced analytics solving the challenge of retail price optimisation using the Same techniques: Pricing elasticity models, optimisation models, competitor Pricing models, etc. The difference lies in the operations workflow, with embedded advanced analytics eliminating manual updates and multiple interfaces.

Advanced Analytics vs Embedded Advanced Analytics for Insurance Pricing

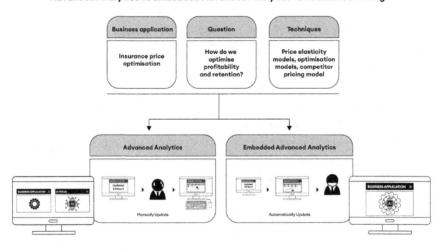

FIGURE 3.4 Hierarchical diagram showing advanced analytics and embedded advanced analytics solving the challenges of insurance premium optimisation using the Same techniques: Pricing elasticity models, optimisation models, competitor Pricing models, etc. The difference lies in the operations workflow, with embedded advanced analytics eliminating cognitive loading and tough decision-making for sales teams in call centres.

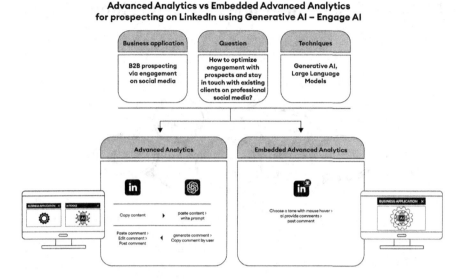

FIGURE 3.5   Hierarchical diagram showing engage AI as an embedded advanced analytics solution versus using advanced analytics tools to Prospect on LinkedIn. The difference lies in the user workflow, with engaged AI being embedded in the lead nurturing process to eliminate additional writing and clicks that take up precious time.

Illustrations: Real-World Use Cases

In the field of advanced analytics, companies from various industries have successfully embedded advanced analytics into their operations, leading to significant benefits. Through these cutting-edge integrations, these companies create value, enhance customer experiences and manage risks more effectively. In this section, we will explore three real-world examples demonstrating the power and potential of embedded advanced analytics.

Dynamic Pricing

Dynamic pricing, an excellent example of embedding advanced analytics into pricing strategies, involves using advanced analytics algorithms to adjust prices in near real-time based on factors like demand, competition and market conditions. The airline industry and e-commerce giant Amazon, among others, employ dynamic pricing strategies to optimise their revenue streams.

As shown in Figure 3.6, airlines continuously adjust ticket prices based on seat availability, time until departure and competitor pricing, optimising revenue by encouraging early bookings and enforcing premium

Dynamic Pricing in Airlines Revenue Management

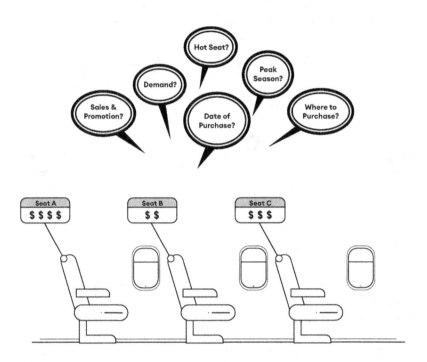

FIGURE 3.6 Seats in an aeroplane with different price tags depending on various factors: Sales and promotion, demand, Date of purchase, purchase location, season and hot seat.

pricing for last-minute buyers. Similarly, Amazon employs a dynamic pricing model that adjusts product prices in real-time, reflecting supply, demand and competitor pricing changes. By embedding advanced analytics into their pricing systems, both industries optimise revenue generation while remaining competitive in their respective markets.

Recommendation Systems in Social Media and Streaming Platforms
Recommendation systems rely on advanced analytics techniques to provide social media and streaming platform users with personalised content suggestions. By employing techniques like collaborative filtering, content-based filtering and deep learning, these services can provide relevant recommendations based on their users' preferences, behaviour and interaction history.

Recommendation Systems in Streaming Platforms

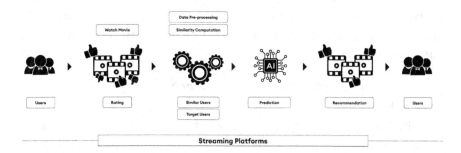

FIGURE 3.7   Image showing how recommendation systems on streaming platforms work. From watching a movie, the AI predicts and recommends similar content that the users May enjoy.

Subsequently, social media and streaming platforms enhance customer experiences and increase user engagement. Streaming platforms like Netflix and Spotify use advanced analytics to recommend movies, TV shows and music tailored to each user's unique tastes, keeping them engaged and encouraging prolonged usage. Meanwhile, social media platforms like Facebook and Twitter utilise advanced analytics algorithms to curate personalised content feeds that align with users' interests and preferences, delivering a more engaging and enjoyable experience. Figure 3.7 shows how the AI provides movie recommendations to a user by making predictions based on one movie they chose to view.

Advanced Analytics in Credit Card Fraud Detection

The application of advanced analytics in credit card fraud detection demonstrates its role in managing risk. Financial institutions and credit card companies embed advanced analytics into their fraud detection systems, improving their ability to detect and prevent fraudulent transactions.

By analysing large volumes of transactional data and identifying patterns and anomalies indicative of fraud, advanced algorithms can accurately flag suspicious transactions in near real-time, enabling swift action and minimising losses. Integrating advanced analytics enhances the accuracy and efficiency of fraud detection systems, helping organisations better manage risk and safeguard their customers.

These real-world examples highlight the transformative potential of embedded advanced analytics in various aspects of an organisation's operations. By integrating advanced analytics into pricing strategies, customer experiences and risk management systems, companies can optimise their operations, generate value and maintain a competitive edge in today's business landscape.

Barriers to Implementing Embedded Advanced Analytics in Organisations

With increasingly apparent benefits to adopting embedded advanced analytics, it is natural to wonder about the lack of widespread adoption. In this section, we will discuss the challenges that hinder organisations from embracing this approach and their implications for organisations looking to embed advanced analytics into their daily operations. We look at this in more detail in Chapters 5–9 and propose a pragmatic approach to overcome this scepticism and build trust.

Scepticism and Confusion around Data Analytics and Advanced Analytics

To iterate one of the more common challenges in the industry, some executives remain sceptical or confused about the distinction between data analytics and advanced analytics. The lack of understanding of advanced analytics' potential benefits and unique capabilities compared to traditional data analytics methods may lead to reluctance to invest in the necessary infrastructure, resources and training required for effective implementation.

Data Quality and Trust Issues

Ensuring accurate, reliable and up-to-date data is complex and time-consuming. Organisations lacking robust data governance practices may find building trust in their data challenging, impeding the adoption of advanced analytics solutions.

Past Negative Experiences

Previous large, unsuccessful advanced analytics projects can discourage organisations from attempting new implementations. Poorly executed or overly ambitious projects create a perception that advanced analytics initiatives are inherently risky and prone to failure. Overcoming this perception and securing buy-in and stakeholder support for new projects can be a significant challenge.

Limitations of Legacy Systems

Embedding advanced analytics into existing operations can be challenging for organisations relying on outdated and inflexible legacy systems. Integrating these systems with modern analytics tools requires substantial time and money, making it a barrier for organisations with limited resources or competing priorities.

Lack of Talent and Skill

When there is a scarcity of professionals with the requisite skills and knowledge in the organisation, it is hard to bridge the gap between business and technical aspects of advanced analytics. Implementing embedded advanced analytics requires a deep understanding of both the organisation's business processes and the supporting technical systems. Finding talent with this unique combination of skills can take time and effort, making it difficult to build a convincing business case for investment.

To overcome the challenges reiterated in Figure 3.8, organisations must invest in education, infrastructure and talent development. Establishing a data governance framework, fostering a culture of innovation and adaptability, and prioritising the integration of advanced analytics capabilities within legacy systems can help address these barriers. By adhering to these best practices, organisations can unlock the full potential of embedded advanced analytics and enjoy improved decision-making, enhanced customer experiences and optimised operations.

Barriers and Challenges in Embedding Advanced Analytics

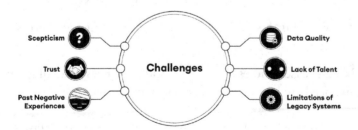

FIGURE 3.8 Challenges in embedding advanced analytics: Scepticism, trust, past negative experiences, data quality, lack of talent and limitations of legacy systems.

Forging the Path Ahead: Building Advanced Analytics for Now
and the Future

Now that we have explored the challenges and future directions of advanced analytics, it begs the question: How can we actively shape the development of advanced analytics to cater to both the present and future demands?

The shift in buying power towards the younger generation has long been observed over recent years. Consumers today are highly exposed and accustomed to the personalised and seamless experiences Big Tech companies provide, elevating their expectations of software, AI and technology. Hence, it is inevitable that organisations re-evaluate their customer experience strategies and seek new ways to enhance their offerings to meet the younger generation's heightened expectations. After all, these organisations will not only be competing with other businesses within a single industry. Instead, they would be going up against a much steeper benchmark and competing against the best experiences offered by tech giants.

While data and advanced analytics alone do not guarantee success, organisations that strategically leverage these tools can gain a competitive edge. By integrating advanced analytics into their operations, businesses can improve customer service, optimise cost management, increase productivity and attract top talent. These optimisations will then contribute to a superior profit margin and enhanced customer experience.

In the upcoming chapters, we will:

- Explore strategies to help organisations navigate the transition to advanced analytics successfully

- Address challenges associated with implementing embedded advanced analytics

- Discuss the importance of fostering a data-driven culture

- Discuss the importance of investing in the necessary infrastructure and talent

- Explore case studies and real-world examples that illustrate how advanced analytics drives business transformation

As the business landscape continues to evolve, the importance of data and advanced analytics will only grow. Organisations that effectively transition to advanced analytics, embedding these tools into their operations, will be well-prepared to thrive in this era of data-driven decision-making. By embracing advanced analytics, businesses can unlock untapped potential, drive innovation and position themselves for sustainable growth and long-term success.

A Comprehensive Approach to Embedding Advanced Analytics

In the following chapters, we will delve into the essential aspects of successfully implementing advanced analytics in organisations. We will utilise two distinct frameworks: The technical implementation framework and the organisational implementation framework.

Technical Implementation Framework

The technical implementation framework will be a comprehensive guide for integrating advanced analytics into your organisation's existing technology stack. We will discuss best practices for effective data management, solution development, infrastructure planning and system architecture. Additionally, we will provide insights into selecting suitable analytics tools and technologies and offer strategies for ensuring seamless integration with your current systems. We explore the technical implementation framework in detail in Chapter 4 – A Step-by-Step Framework for Embedding Advanced Analytics.

Organisational Implementation Framework

On the other hand, the organisational implementation framework will address the critical non-technical aspects of embedding advanced analytics into your organisation's culture and processes. This will include topics such as change management, leadership, team structure and skill development. We will also discuss approaches to fostering a data-driven culture and aligning analytics initiatives with your overall business objectives. We explore these topics and introduce a practical approach to the organisational implementation in Chapters 5–12.

Converged Approach

By combining these two frameworks, organisations can develop a holistic strategy for successfully implementing advanced analytics. This comprehensive approach ensures that both the technical and non-technical aspects are considered, maximising the potential benefits and driving transformative change throughout the organisation.

Whether you are focusing on the technical framework, the organisational framework, or the holistic approach, our discussions will equip you with the knowledge and tools needed to navigate the complex landscape of advanced analytics implementation.

CHAPTER **4**

A Step-by-Step Framework for Embedding Advanced Analytics

4.1 IMPLEMENTATION CHALLENGES FACED BY CHIEF DATA AND ANALYTICS OFFICERS

To clearly illustrate the challenges of organisations aiming to implement advanced analytics, we will introduce Simon, our avatar modelled after the typical CDAO.

Simon holds the position of CDAO at a large integrated healthcare company in the United Kingdom. He oversees a Data Science Centre of Excellence, providing guidance and support to various business units within his organisation.

Unfortunately, Simon finds himself constantly frustrated with the limited impact of the analytics work produced by his team. Despite their efforts, their analytics projects never progress beyond the stage of flashy dashboards and PowerPoint presentations.

Like countless other CDAOs, Simon's exasperation stems from his unfruitful attempts to translate the promised value of their analytical models into practical implementation. To fully unleash the transformative potential of their analytics models, Simon needs to work with the IT department to

DOI: 10.1201/9781003408222-4

change their enterprise IT systems. Alternatively, he must rely on the front-line staff to meticulously follow manual instructions.

Unfortunately, these implementation efforts tend to drag on indefinitely or, worse yet, never materialise at all. This challenge is widespread among CDAOs across various organisations, especially ones from large enterprises and government agencies with extensive IT teams and multiple enterprise systems. Despite their genuine desire to establish a data-driven company, the practical application of a data-driven philosophy proves an arduous task when dealing with enterprise systems.

There is a solution to solve this problem, however, and various organisations have implemented it successfully. The key to achieving success like those organisations is to steer clear of developing an advanced analytics platform that relies on interactions with enterprise systems and enterprise IT teams for its recommendations.

Instead, the optimal approach is to build an independent advanced analytics platform situated outside of enterprise systems. With this setup, the output generated by the advanced analytics platform can be seamlessly integrated into the enterprise systems as valuable data.

Based on the diagram in Figure 4.1, there are many elements involved in building an advanced analytics platform. To understand the relationships between those components, we will first explore each of them separately.

ERPS: Their Role in Enterprises and Government Agencies

Enterprises and government agencies worldwide typically rely on core Enterprise Systems (ES) or Enterprise Resource Planning (ERP) solutions to manage daily operations and serve customers effectively. These comprehensive systems, procured from leading software vendors, are designed to streamline business processes across various functions such as finance, supply chain management, human resources and customer relationship management.

To ensure that the ES or ERP aligns with their specific business requirements, organisations often engage in customisation. This process involves making adjustments and incorporating additional functionalities into the system. Collaborating with software vendors, third-party consultants or in-house IT teams, organisations modify the ERP solution to meet their unique needs and industry best practices.

The customisation process begins with thoroughly analysing the organisation's existing business processes. This assessment helps identify areas where the standard functionality of the ES or ERP may require

Traditional Means of Developing the Advanced Analytics Platform

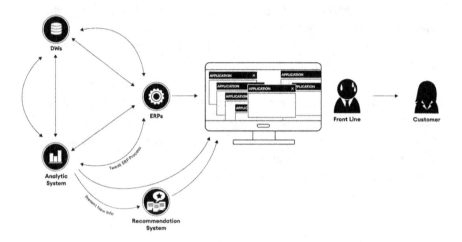

FIGURE 4.1 Multiple components in building an advanced analytics platform, including data warehouses, Enterprise resource planning and analytics system, lead to workload increase for both data teams and frontline customer support agents.

improvement. By understanding these gaps, organisations can tailor the system to enhance operational efficiency, optimise resource utilisation and deliver better customer value.

Data Warehouse Development

A well-designed data warehouse provides a robust, scalable infrastructure that facilitates efficient storage, retrieval and analysis of large volumes of data. It forms the foundation of advanced analytics, enabling organisations to uncover patterns, trends and relationships that drive informed decision-making and strategic planning.

To extract maximum value from the data generated by their ERP systems, enterprises commonly employ Extract, Transform and Load (ETL) or Extract, Load and Transform (ELT) processes. These ETL or ELT processes involve consolidating data from various sources, including ERP systems, internal systems, websites, CRM platforms and IoT devices.

Once the data has been extracted from these sources, it undergoes a transformation process. This step involves cleaning, standardising and restructuring the data to ensure consistency and compatibility. By improving data quality, organisations can ascertain the validity and reliability of the stored information within the data warehouse.

Following the transformation process, the cleaned and structured data is loaded into the data warehouse to provide one unified, holistic view of their operations. Overall, data unification enables a deeper understanding of customers, operations and market dynamics, facilitating optimisation and differentiation in the competitive business landscape.

Analytics Systems Development

After successfully consolidating data from multiple sources into a single data warehouse, enterprises can leverage advanced analytics systems to perform a wide range of functions. As discussed in an earlier chapter, advanced analytics employs sophisticated techniques and tools to analyse data, extract insights and make data-driven decisions. It surpasses traditional business intelligence and reporting by leveraging techniques like machine learning, predictive modelling and data mining.

We summarise the use of advanced analytics under several key areas:

1. **Predictive analytics:** Predictive analytics utilises historical data to predict future events or outcomes. It allows organisations to anticipate customer behaviour and demands as well as potential risks. For example, retailers can optimise inventory levels based on sales forecasts.

2. **Prescriptive analytics:** Prescriptive analytics goes a step further by recommending specific actions to achieve desired outcomes. It combines predictive analytics with optimisation algorithms to suggest the best course of action. For instance, logistics companies can optimise delivery routes to reduce fuel costs.

3. **Customer analytics:** Advanced analytics enables organisations to better understand their customers by analysing data from various sources such as transaction records and social media. This helps businesses segment customers, personalise marketing campaigns and improve customer experience.

4. **Fraud detection:** Advanced analytics can identify unusual patterns and anomalies in data that may indicate fraudulent activities. Financial institutions use machine learning algorithms to detect credit card fraud, insurance fraud and other forms of financial crimes.

5. **Operations optimisation:** Advanced analytics can improve operational efficiency by identifying bottlenecks, optimising resource allocation and automating repetitive tasks. For example, manufacturers can use advanced analytics to optimise production schedules and reduce downtime.

6. **Risk management:** Advanced analytics helps organisations assess and mitigate risks by analysing large volumes of data from various sources. It enables businesses to identify potential threats, assess their impact and take proactive measures to minimise risk exposure.

4.2 DRIVING ADOPTION OF ANALYTICS SYSTEMS: CONVENTIONAL APPROACHES

There are currently three approaches that analytics professionals use to encourage the adoption of analytics:

- **Approach 1:** Utilise PowerPoint presentations and business intelligence dashboards to persuade C-level executives to implement changes in business strategy or ES.

- **Approach 2:** Present the analytics results in a separate system accessible to frontline employees, expecting them to follow the instructions provided diligently.

- **Approach 3:** Collaborate with enterprise IT teams to consistently incorporate recommendations from analytics output into the ongoing development and adjustments of ERP systems.

Approach 1

The PowerPoint presentations meant to convince C-level executives are often neglected and left to gather dust. It could take months before the executive management team reads them. Coordinating multiple teams and personnel to agree on proposed changes can also take a significant amount of time. Consequently, when these changes are finally implemented, they are already several months or even years behind more advanced competitors.

Approach 2

As shown in Figure 4.2, a primary challenge frontline employees face is navigating and retrieving information from multiple systems while

Approach 2 to Displaying Recommendation to Employees

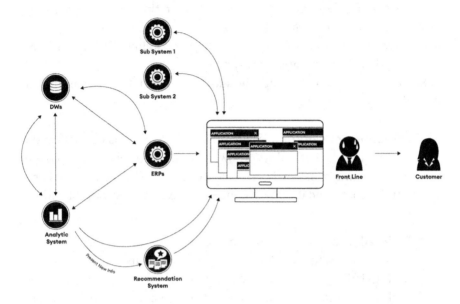

FIGURE 4.2   Front-facing customer service staff face complications as advanced analytics systems add to the list of applications they must cross-reference while addressing customer inquiries.

serving clients. This challenge is intensified if front-facing customer service staff must adhere to complicated instructions for each system and deal with demanding customers who expect immediate results while navigating multiple systems.

Unfortunately, employees stationed at headquarters often underestimate the energy and effort frontline staff require to serve customers effectively. As they are distant from the problem, there is a lack of understanding and empathy. This, combined with poor system design and the complexity of navigating multiple systems, contributes to the low levels of customer satisfaction experienced by call centres. Evidently, the sheer amount of customer issues and inquiries to resolve within a limited timeframe leaves little room for frontline staff to go above and beyond. With so much to do, impressing customers with insights derived from analytics systems is simply out of reach.

Remember: Without embedding advanced analytics into existing operational processes, an organisation may possess valuable data but struggle to capitalise on its full potential and achieve tangible business accounts. As mentioned above, employees must navigate various systems to extract information. In other words, they view the analytical model's results and recommendations on multiple screens. The time-consuming process makes it less likely for employees to leverage and follow through with recommendations from the analytics systems.

Some barriers that discourage the adoption of analytics systems include the following:

1. **Disruption of workflow:** Switching between screens or applications can disrupt the natural workflow of frontline employees. Having to navigate away from their primary work environment to access analytics recommendations introduces friction and resistance to adopting these suggestions.

2. **Reduced context:** Viewing the recommendations on a separate screen can result in a loss of context. Frontline employees might find it challenging to understand how the recommendations relate to their specific tasks or activities when they are not seamlessly integrated into the systems they use daily.

3. **Cognitive overload:** Managing multiple screens and applications increases cognitive load, making it harder for employees to process and retain information. As a result, they may become overwhelmed, impeding their ability to incorporate analytics recommendations into their decision-making processes effectively.

4. **Inefficiency:** Accessing recommendations on a separate screen can introduce inefficiencies in the employees' work processes. Time spent switching between screens or applications will accumulate, reducing overall productivity and diminishing the potential benefits of analytics insights.

5. **Decreased engagement:** Presenting recommendations on a separate screen creates a sense of detachment for frontline employees, diminishing their engagement and connection. This detachment results in a lack of ownership and commitment when implementing suggested actions.

To conclude, it is crucial to integrate the insights into existing systems and workflows. By embedding recommendations directly within the tools and platforms employees use daily, organisations can enhance the relevance, accessibility and effectiveness of analytics-driven insights. This integration subsequently empowers frontline staff to make more informed decisions and optimise their work processes while mitigating the obstacles posed by navigating multiple systems.

Approach 3

While there are analytics teams collaborating closely with enterprise teams to implement changes in ERP systems, organisations often make a critical mistake when it comes to the system design for integrating analytics and ERP. As shown in Figure 4.3, this mistake involves an unending cycle of modifying IT processes or workflows within the ERP, which introduces complications and conflicts of interest.

The interests of analytics professionals and ERP teams are misaligned. The primary responsibility of ERP systems is to ensure smooth operations and customer service. Consequently, any additional changes required for analytics integration become lesser priorities subjected to meticulous analysis to prevent disruptions to the ERP system. As a result, every change requested by analytics professionals typically takes months to implement.

Approach 3 – Constantly Tweaking ERP Process and System

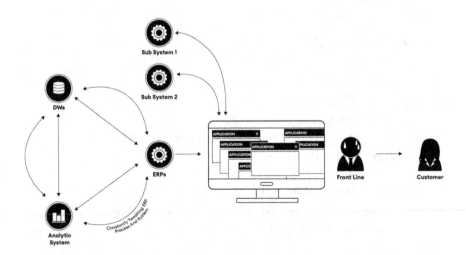

FIGURE 4.3 Data teams constantly tweak the ERP processes and systems to accommodate analytics recommendations.

Modifying ERPs or developing custom connectors introduces various complications, including:

1. **Increased complexity:** As organisations continuously modify the ERP system to accommodate analytics recommendations, the system may become more complex and difficult to manage. This increased complexity poses a higher risk of errors, system downtime or unintended consequences that may impact other areas of the ERP system.

2. **Maintenance challenges:** Each modification adds to the burden of maintaining and troubleshooting the ERP system. IT teams may struggle to keep up with the growing demands of maintaining a heavily customised system while ensuring stability and efficiency.

3. **Organisational resistance:** Constant changes to the ERP system can lead to resistance from employees who must adapt to new processes and workflows. This resistance hampers the adoption of analytics-driven improvements and limits the overall effectiveness of integration efforts.

4. **Reduced agility:** As the ERP system becomes increasingly customised, its flexibility and adaptability to future changes diminish. This reduced agility restricts an organisation's ability to respond to evolving business needs or take advantage of new technologies and opportunities.

4.3 DRIVING ADOPTION OF ADVANCED ANALYTICS SYSTEMS: MODERN APPROACH

Previously, we explored the traditional approaches to driving the adoption of advanced analytics systems. In this section, we will take on a contemporary approach where organisations can seamlessly integrate recommendations and insights into their existing systems and workflows.

The approach is built upon three key principles:

Principle 1: Minimal Effort and Cognitive Loading

Recommendations and predictions from the advanced analytics systems should seamlessly integrate into existing processes without requiring frontline employees to exert additional effort or interpret complex information. By embedding recommendations directly into the workflow, employees can easily follow suggestions without cognitive overload.

Principle 2: Minimal Process and Workflow Changes

Recommendations and predictions should only update the data in the ERP system's database rather than altering entire processes and workflows. This is, of course, with the exception of the initial implementation of such advanced analytics systems.

Principle 3: Autonomy and Collaboration

It may seem like an oxymoron, but it is important that individuals who work together also maintain some semblance of autonomy or independence. Data scientists and ERP teams should work independently on their respective systems, leveraging their core skill sets and expertise with minimal interference from the other team.

By following key principles in implementing advanced analytics, organisations can achieve tangible outcomes that enhance their IT systems and operations:

Outcome 1: Independent Advanced Analytics Platform

Developing the advanced analytics platform outside the enterprise system allows data scientists to continuously build, test and benchmark new models without relying heavily on the IT enterprise team. This autonomy allows for faster experimentation and adaptation while minimising disruptions to the enterprise system.

Outcome 2: Data-Driven Updates

Data-driven updates simplify the integration process and reduce the complications of altering the enterprise system. By establishing a seamless data update process, the advanced analytics system can consistently integrate insights without frequent intervention from the IT enterprise team.

Outcome 3: Actionable Insights

Frontline employees can easily understand and implement analytics insights without the need to decipher complex information. These insights and recommendations are presented as specific and actionable steps or decisions, enabling frontline employees to enhance their decision-making and streamline their workflows.

Let us use pricing analytics as an example. Instead of expecting frontline employees to estimate discounts, this approach gives them a precise discounted price based on the probability of retaining a customer at a given discount level.

Modern Approach to Integrate Advanced Analytics

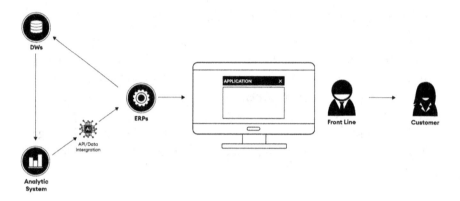

FIGURE 4.4   API/data integration simplifies the workload of data teams and frontline employees.

As the macro environment changes for the enterprise system in an industry, the above principles become even more vital.

As seen in Figure 4.4, this is particularly relevant when integrating generative AI into ERP systems, where both the input data and output recommendations are unstructured. Traditional ERP teams and systems are not designed to handle large recommendation volumes generated from unstructured data.

4.4 ENRICHING ERP AND LARGE ENTERPRISE WITH GENERATIVE AI: A COMPREHENSIVE FRAMEWORK FOR DESIGN AND DEVELOPMENT

ChatGPT took the world by storm on 30 November, 2022, revolutionising human-technology interaction and shaping the future of AI. This ground-breaking innovation continues to capture global attention, compelling major technology giants like Google, Facebook and Amazon to scramble and develop their own versions of ChatGPT. Needless to say, each one of them vies for dominance in the rapidly evolving AI landscape, and they are not alone in this endeavour.

Apart from the technology giants, startups and smaller technology companies also recognise the immense potential of ChatGPT. In fact,

Generative AI Integration into the ERP Systems

FIGURE 4.5   Process of generative AI integration: (1) identify business use cases; (2) extract, encode and index data; (3) search, retrieve and re-rank; (4) input results into LLMs and (5) embed LLM-generated recommendations.

many have already started integrating generative AI into their software using the process outlined in Figure 4.5, thereby enhancing customer service experiences and transforming how their businesses operate. It is without question that this powerful AI-driven innovation is not only disrupting the tech industry but also redefining how we perceive and utilise AI in our daily lives.

As its popularity grows, visionaries begin to deliberate ChatGPT's implications for other industries. How does it influence the corporate world and enterprises? What about higher education and government agencies?

ChatGPT's virality has sparked tremendous interest, prompting even business stakeholders to engage their CDAOs to explore the use cases of generative AI and Large Language Models (LLMs) for their organisations.

In the subsequent subsections, we will present a tried-and-tested framework comprising five actionable steps. This framework is derived from our own experiences leveraging generative AI, vector databases, embeddings and LLMs on two fronts:

- Developing Engage AI, a Conversation CoPilot technology assisting technical founders in building relationships and closing more sales effectively

- Developing and deploying generative AI for enterprises

Going forward, it is important to note that the terms ChatGPT, generative AI and LLMs are used interchangeably.

Step 1: Identify Business Use Cases

Consider one purchase that we've made. It should be something we bought simply because everyone around us was getting it, and it remained unused either because it didn't serve any practical purpose for us or because we couldn't figure out how to use it. Humans naturally crave novelty and a sense of belonging; impulse purchases validate those needs. In some cases, the purchases are worthwhile; in others, they're unnecessary expenditures.

Shiny Object Syndrome (SOS) is a persistent state of distraction fuelled by the belief that something new is worth pursuing (*Shiny Object Syndrome*, 2022). At an individual level, the consequences of materialistic indulgence may cause a temporary dent in an individual's finances for a few months. However, the stakes are so much higher on an organisation's scale.

To keep up with the latest trends and technology, organisations are enticed to make technological adoptions first and decide what they will solve for their business later. Such novelties can blindside stakeholders from making informed decisions, especially when driven by fear of falling behind competitors. At the expense of core objectives, existing priorities and long-term goals, these organisations chase the latest trends, leading to wasted resources, time and opportunities.

To avoid the pitfalls of Shiny Object Syndrome, CDAOs and business stakeholders must consult with each other when deploying generative AI into their organisations. During the exploration phase, it is crucial to identify potential use cases.

From our experiences and consultations with other CDAOs, relevant use cases may include the following:

- Existing customer service chatbots improvement

- Rapid knowledge management retrieval for customer queries

- Marketing and sales copy creation

- Conversation CoPilot for customer services

Ways to avoid Shiny Object Syndrome and other common pitfalls are explored in more detail in Chapter 6 – Understand Your Business – Moments that Matter.

Identify Organisational Challenges

The first step to prevent Shiny Object Syndrome is to evaluate the best use case for advanced analytics within your organisation. The Innovation

Ambition Matrix by Bansi Nagji and Geoff Tuff from Harvard Business Review can help with this evaluation.

The Innovation Ambition Matrix consists of three concentric circles (Nagji and Tuff, 2012):

1. **Core:** Innovations that enhance or optimise the organisation's existing products, services, or processes. These incremental improvements align closely with the organisation's current competencies and offerings.

2. **Adjacent:** Innovations that enhance or optimise the organisation's existing products, services, or processes. These incremental improvements align closely with the organisation's current competencies and offerings.

3. **Transformational:** Innovations that represent a significant departure from the organisation's current business model, products or services. These opportunities have the potential for high impact but also carry higher risks and require new competencies.

Organisations can use the Innovation Ambition Matrix to assess and prioritise new technology opportunities based on where they fall within these three categories. This allows for a balanced approach, considering both incremental improvements and transformative innovations.

To best illustrate the use of Innovation Ambition Matrix, we will once again bring in our CDAO persona, Simon, from earlier on in this chapter. After negotiating with business stakeholders and conducting an evaluation with the Innovation Ambition Matrix, Simon and his organisation settled on the use case of Customer Copilot for customer services.

With organisations striving to meet the customer service benchmark raised by tech giants, Simon's organisation aims to address the following problems for their customer service team:

- Customer service consultants rely on multiple IT systems and communication channels to gather information and make assessments.

- Searching for company policies stored as unstructured data is limited by existing technology.

- Consuming unstructured data such as company policies, phone calls, notes, emails and web chats from customers and consultants is time-consuming and challenging.

- After finding the required information, support consultants need to rephrase policies for individual customers, resulting in repetitive and time-consuming tasks.

- Navigating multiple systems is challenging, and underperforming consultants may miss critical information when supporting customers.

- Maintaining quality customer service while keeping costs down is a critical outcome.

- The high turnover of customer support consultants results in losing intimate knowledge between consultants and clients.

In Chapter 6 – Understand Your Business – Moments that Matter, we explore how this approach can be integrated into the Organisation Implementation Framework to get the best initiative to start your journey.

Decide the Minimum Viable Product (MVP)

With the guidance of external experts experienced in deploying generative AI and LLMs, organisations can decide on an MVP.

In Simon's case, he and his business stakeholders could solve the above problems by combining the following:

- Vector database for storing unstructured data across multiple systems

- Embedding techniques for querying unstructured data

- LLMs to contextualise company policies for customer replies

This approach creates a single touchpoint for customer support consultants, allowing them to:

- Search and query past information across multiple systems.

- Access customer support policies.

- Utilise FAQs in knowledge management.

- Understand customers' context, problems and potential solutions on one screen.

Work Backwards

Once you have identified your business goals for improving analytical capabilities, you will need to know who and what needs to be involved in the process to ensure successful implementation.

While we live in the age of AI, we must recognise that people are still at the core of any successful system. Even the most advanced AI systems rely on high-quality inputs, calling for dedicated individuals' involvement to ensure data quality. Ultimately, the process has no point unless the higher quality data and insights generated lead to tangible business improvements. Thus, staff within the organisation are responsible for bridging the gap between analytics-driven insights and the necessary actions for achieving business benefits.

It is crucial at this stage to also take into account external stakeholders. Consultants with specialised expertise may need to be engaged to support the process, and customers may need to be informed about the potential use of their data. Therefore, a systematic and comprehensive approach is necessary to identify and engage all relevant individuals and stakeholders in the process of embedding advanced analytics.

To achieve this, a carefully designed process should be implemented. As you trace each final use case backwards, consider the following questions:

- Who needs to be involved in each step of the process to make it work, and who will be impacted by it (considering both internal and external stakeholders)?

- Who is responsible for informing and engaging the relevant individuals in the process?

- How can people be best informed or engaged, and what processes need to be in place to facilitate this?

- When should stakeholders be informed and engaged?

- What outputs and outcomes are expected from this engagement, and how will we determine if those expectations have been met?

- What external consultancy expertise might be required at each step of the process?

Once again, we will use Simon's case to give you a better idea of what organisations must consider as important stakeholders in the process.

Simon's organisation chose to focus on the use case of Customer Copilot for customer services. To achieve it, they compiled a (non-exhaustive) list of potential stakeholders they must engage at different process stages.

- The organisation's leadership team
- Customer service managers and consultants
- Senior management and staff from the IT department
- External consultants and/or service providers
- R&D and data science teams
- Knowledge management team
- Company's customers

Simon needs to devise appropriate strategies to engage these stakeholders and involve them in relevant stages of the process while considering the questions outlined above. For example, the leadership team's initial approval of the project and ongoing monitoring may require a lighter touch compared to the detailed engagement with the customer service management, which is crucial for the project's success.

To reiterate, informing and engaging the right people is vital for the technical implementation process. However, people are not the only consideration at this stage. It is also necessary to work backwards from the final use cases to identify the required data and systems that will support the process.

To identify the necessary data and systems, ask similar questions to the ones posed above, but this time with a focus on what is needed:

- What data and systems are required for each step of the process, and which ones will be impacted by it?
- Are the necessary data and systems already in place, and if not, what actions are needed to implement them?
- What changes to existing practices are necessary to ensure that the data and systems are suitable for implementing embedded advanced analytics and generative AI, and achieving the intended use cases?

- When will the data or system be required or impacted, and what additional work is necessary for optimal process efficiency?

- What outputs and outcomes are expected from interacting with the required data and systems, and how will the fulfilment of these expectations be measured?

Using Simon's healthcare organisation example, some of the required data and systems to introduce generative AI might include:

- General company policies

- Knowledge management policies

- Curated FAQs

- Core ERP and CRM data

- Product information

- Customer information

- Billing information

- Notes in ERPs

- Internal and external notes

- Emails

- Transcripts of phone calls, web chats and chat applications

This is not an exhaustive list but provides an overview of the types and volume of data to be identified during this stage. To comprehensively identify the required data, it is helpful to consider two categories: Structured and unstructured data. These categories are explained in more detail in Step 3, which focuses on the data collection process illustrated in Figure 4.6.

Step 2: Extract, Encode and Index: Structured and Unstructured Data

In advanced analytics, data is the vital fuel that powers the system. This holds equally true for generative AI. The adage "garbage in, garbage out" holds particularly true in this context. Without high-quality and relevant

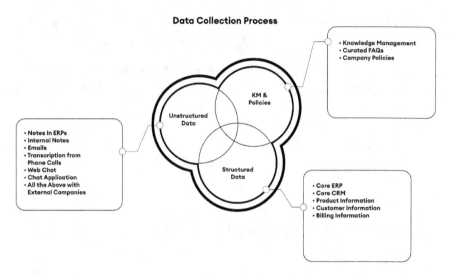

FIGURE 4.6 The data collection process involves unstructured data, structured data and knowledge management and policies.

data, even the most sophisticated AI models become ineffective and incapable of generating meaningful or valuable outputs.

Broadly speaking, data can be categorised into three main categories:

- Unstructured data 1: Company policy or knowledge management

- Unstructured data 2: Past and present customer inquiries

- Structured data: Customer, product/service and other records

As we delve into the technical implementation framework in this chapter, we will explore the importance of data collection in more depth, focusing on both structured and unstructured data as shown in Figure 4.7. We will discuss strategies for identifying, collecting and preparing data to ensure that generative AI models have the strongest possible foundation for learning. This will lay the groundwork for subsequent steps in the implementation process, including model development, training, deployment and integration.

Unstructured Data: Company Policy or Knowledge Management
LLMs thrive on a rich and diverse dataset, which serves as the raw material for learning, adapting and generating novel outputs. The data quality

Extract, Encode and Index Data

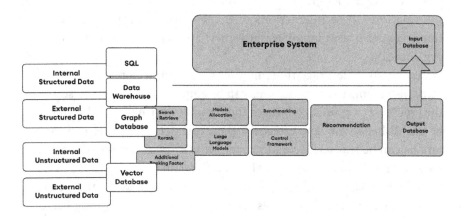

FIGURE 4.7 First step of the technical implementation framework: Extract, encode and index structured and unstructured data.

directly impacts the accuracy and usefulness of the results produced by these LLMs. In this regard, data is not merely an input but a critical asset that significantly influences the success of generative AI projects.

In the present age, organisations of all sizes have greater accessibility to implementing LLMs and generative AI. However, the true differentiating factor lies in the data quality used for training and generating outputs. This holds especially true for unstructured data, which often forms the bulk of knowledge management systems.

Unstructured data like text documents, emails and social media posts contains a wealth of valuable information. It holds insights into customer behaviour, market trends, operational efficiencies and more. Yet, analysing this data using traditional methods can be challenging due to its messy nature. With their ability to understand and generate human-like text, generative AI models are uniquely positioned to unlock the hidden value within unstructured data.

Effectively harnessing unstructured data can provide a significant competitive advantage, enabling organisations to make more accurate predictions, informed decisions and drive better business outcomes. However, the key to unlocking this potential lies in data quality. High-quality and well-curated unstructured data acts as the fuel that empowers generative AI models to deliver transformative results.

Unstructured Data: Past and Present Customer Inquiries

Customer inquiries, regardless of their form – emails, phone calls, web chats, messages, letters, or in-person discussions – are a goldmine of information. These interactions offer real-world examples of the questions, concerns and language customers use when engaging with your organisation.

To effectively leverage these inquiries, the initial step is to collect and centralise them. Various methods can be employed based on the source of the inquiry. For emails, web chats and messages, an automated system can be established to save and categorise these interactions. Phone-call conversations can be transcribed and stored, while in-person discussions can be recorded and summarised by trained staff members.

Once the data is collected, it must undergo processing and preparation before training. This entails cleaning the data, anonymising personal information and formatting it in a manner that is comprehensible to the AI system. An effective approach is to break down each interaction into a series of exchanges, where each exchange comprises a customer input and its corresponding response.

This processed data is an ideal training dataset for conversational AI systems that efficiently respond to customer inquiries. Customer inquiries are crucial in constructing a Conversation CoPilot, providing context for responding to customers using generative AI. The system learns from the examples within the training data, enabling it to respond to various customer inputs. Over time, the system can be fine-tuned and improved based on feedback and additional data.

By adhering to the following step-by-step guide, large enterprises can effectively collect unstructured data and incorporate it into their data lake, data lakehouse and advanced analytics systems (e.g., Conversation CoPilot):

1. **Identify data needs and objectives:** Start by determining the specific unstructured data sources that will provide the most value for your business. Align the data needs with your organisation's objectives and identify the data types that can help address specific challenges or opportunities.

2. **Evaluate data sources:** Research and evaluate potential unstructured data sources based on factors like data quality, relevance, timeliness and cost.

3. **Establish data partnerships and agreements:** Negotiate terms and conditions with internal stakeholders for data sources requiring agreements or partnerships. These talks ensure alignment with your organisation's data usage policies and regulatory compliance requirements.

4. **Develop a data ingestion strategy:** Design a plan outlining how unstructured data will be collected and integrated into your existing systems. Depending on the data source, this may involve using APIs, integrations or data file transfers.

5. **Implement data integration tools:** Utilise data integration tools and technologies like ETL (extract, transform, load) or ELT (extract, load, transform) tools, data lakes, or data warehouses to automate and streamline the process of combining external data with internal data.

6. **Ensure data quality:** Implement data quality management processes to validate, cleanse and enrich external data. This may involve techniques such as data profiling, deduplication, standardisation and enrichment to ensure the data's accuracy, consistency and completeness.

7. **Address data privacy and security concerns:** Develop and enforce data privacy and security policies to protect sensitive unstructured data and comply with relevant regulations. Implement access controls, data encryption and data anonymisation techniques to safeguard the data and maintain privacy.

8. **Monitor and update data sources:** Regularly monitor and evaluate the performance of unstructured data sources to ensure ongoing value for your organisation. Update or replace data sources as needed to maintain data quality and relevance.

Structured Data: Customer, Product/Service and Other Records

In generative AI, the significance of structured data cannot be overstated. While unstructured data like knowledge management assets and customer inquiries provide valuable qualitative insights, structured data offers equally critical quantitative metrics. These structured data points, often related to customers and their purchases of products or services, form the backbone of many analytics operations.

Structured data is organised and easily searchable by nature, making it a valuable resource for any AI system. It provides clear and quantifiable information about customer behaviour, preferences and trends. This includes data points such as purchase history, customer demographics and product preferences. When effectively utilised, this data offers a comprehensive understanding of the customer, guiding strategic decision-making and fuelling business growth.

Data Loading into Vector Database for Embedding (Encode and Index)
Traditionally, data warehouses typically neglect unstructured data due to limitations in the existing data management and warehouse systems. The concept of a data warehouse itself does not support unstructured data. As a result, a vector database is necessary to store unstructured data. Likewise, to fully leverage the potential of structured data, it is crucial to incorporate it into the broader data ecosystem. One effective method involves extracting the structured data from the data warehouse and importing it into a vector database.

A vector database – also referred to as a neural database or embedding database – stores information in the form of vectors. Each vector holds high-dimensional data comprising various features or attributes. Depending on data complexity and granularity, the dimensions of each vector can vary from a few tens to thousands.

Typically, the transformation or embedding of raw data like text, images, audio and video creates these vectors. Experts utilise techniques like machine learning models, word embeddings and feature extraction algorithms to accomplish this.

According to Microsoft, a vector database's primary advantage lies in its ability to facilitate quick and accurate searching and retrieval of data based on the similarity or distance between vectors (Chaki and Bolaños, 2023). Instead of relying on conventional methods that involve exact matches or predefined criteria for querying databases, a vector database allows organisations to identify the most similar or relevant data by considering its semantic or contextual meaning. This process is commonly known as neural search and is especially valuable when working with unstructured data, which often contains detailed and nuanced information that is difficult to quantify or categorise easily (Woodie, 2023).

With the hype surrounding LLMs, few truly grasp the core of many current innovations – the vector database. After all, the unique architecture and capabilities of vector databases make them an ideal choice for handling the high-dimensional data that underpins advanced AI applications.

Within this space, a diverse range of providers exists, offering both open-source solutions and managed services. During our exploration and implementation of vector databases for our own organisation and clients, we have discovered the following companies:

- Weaviate
- Zilliz
- Qdrant
- Vespa
- Chroma
- Marqo.ai
- Pipecone

Structured and Unstructured Data Integration

The vector database assumes the role of long-term memory, capable of accommodating large volumes of unstructured data both in the present and over time. Moreover, its ability to handle high-dimensional data makes it an efficient storage and retrieval solution for structured data, facilitating rapid, near real-time analytics. By integrating these two data types into the vector database, we can create a unified data repository that is both comprehensive and accessible.

It is important to note that loading structured and unstructured data into a vector database requires meticulous planning and execution. The initial step involves preprocessing the data to ensure its compatibility with the chosen format. For structured data, this may entail normalising numerical values and encoding categorical variables. On the other hand, unstructured data may require the utilisation of neural networks to convert the information into vector representations.

Once appropriately formatted, the data can be loaded into the vector database. The process can vary depending on the chosen database system, but it typically involves scripting or employing a database management tool for data import. It is crucial to validate the accuracy of data loading to maintain data integrity and optimise performance.

The final step involves indexing the data to facilitate efficient retrieval. Indexing organises the data in a manner that enables swift and efficient search operations. This step holds particular importance in vector databases, as the high-dimensional nature of the data can result in computationally intensive searches.

To conclude, integrating structured and unstructured data is a pivotal step in implementing generative AI. It enables a nuanced understanding of customers by combining qualitative insights from unstructured data with quantitative metrics from structured data. Consequently, the AI system can generate more accurate and relevant outputs, driving tangible business value.

Step 3: Search, Retrieve and Re-rank

Once the data has been extracted, encoded and indexed, the subsequent step involves data search and retrieval, as seen in Figure 4.8. Regardless of how effectively the preceding steps were executed, establishing efficient and accurate methods for retrieving the most relevant data is crucial for analysis and utilisation. In this regard, it is crucial to grasp yet another key distinction between vector databases and traditional databases: The use of similarity metrics.

Whereas traditional databases primarily employ exact-match queries to search through predefined indexes, vector databases allow similarity searches, which examine vectors to identify data that closely resembles the query. To achieve that, vector databases employ mathematical techniques that leverage similarity metrics, also known as similarity measures,

Search, Retrieve and Rerank

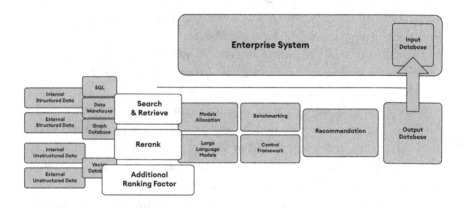

FIGURE 4.8 Second step of the technical implementation framework: Search, retrieve and re-rank data.

to determine the degree of similarity between two vectors. Thus, a vector database can compare possible results and pinpoint the most relevant answers whenever it receives a query input.

Similarity searches are especially useful for complex AI tasks in which approximate matches can be more relevant than exact ones. When queries are subjective and have multiple possible answers, the model must be able to grasp the deeper conceptual meaning and retrieve information after sifting through billions of objects. Remember the dialogue between a user and its AI companion in Chapter 1? One user may search "What apples should I buy?" whereas another may search "What Apple product should I buy?"

To humans, it is obvious that the former user is referring to the fruit and the other to the brand. However, the AI model must discern between the two terms, comprehend the subtle nuances and return results tailored to the user's intent. Thus, by employing similarity searches, it can analyse the input, identify similar items and provide the user with relevant information.

Vector databases employ a range of similarity metrics to facilitate effective and rapid data retrieval. Some of the most common ones include the following:

- **Cosine similarity:** This metric takes two vectors and measures the cosine of the angle between them. It generates results ranging from 1 to -1, with 1 indicating identical vectors, -1 indicating diametrically opposed vectors, and 0 signifying orthogonal vectors. Orthogonal vectors have a relationship exactly midway between being identical and entirely different.

- **Dot product similarity:** Similar to cosine similarity, this metric also measures the cosine of the angle between two vectors. However, it also measures the sum of two vectors' magnitudes. Its range extends from $-\infty$ to ∞, with a positive value indicating vectors pointing in the same direction and a negative value indicating vectors pointing in opposite directions. Again, as with cosine similarity, 0 indicates orthogonal vectors.

- **Euclidean distance:** This metric calculates the straight-line distance between two vectors. In contrast to cosine similarity, the range of Euclidean distance starts from 0 and goes up to infinity. A value of 0 indicates identical vectors, while higher values indicate increasing dissimilarity between the vectors.

Naturally, each similarity metric has its own strengths and weaknesses. Your choice of metric will impact the results obtained during searches. Some factors to consider when selecting a metric:

- Cosine similarity is generally well-suited for semantic searches and problems involving document classification since it compares the overall directions of vectors. However, it may not be suitable for searches where the magnitude of each vector holds significance due to its focus on direction.

- Dot product similarity is commonly utilised for training LLMs, making it a suitable metric for such models. Generally, the metric used for training the system tends to be the most effective for data search and retrieval.

- Euclidean distance's sensitivity to magnitudes makes it a suitable metric when searching for information relating to counting and numerical measurement. However, its simplicity relative to other metrics makes it less appropriate for deep learning models, which often require more complex representations.

Efficient and accurate searches in vector databases are achieved through utilising various algorithms that contribute to an approximate nearest neighbour search. These algorithms, including quantisation, space partition and graph-based searching, work in tandem to optimise the search process (Chen et al., n.d.).

The combination of these algorithms forms a pipeline that swiftly and precisely retrieves the nearest neighbours of the queried vector. However, it is important to acknowledge that trade-offs between speed and accuracy can exist in vector databases. In other words, the speed at which the search process is executed may impact the results' accuracy. Nonetheless, modern systems have made remarkable progress, capable of striking a balance between near-perfect accuracy and ultra-fast performance.

The search and retrieval process for data in vector databases can be summarised as follows:

1. **Generate vector embeddings:** Begin by taking the desired content and utilising an embedding model to create vector embeddings.

2. **Insert embeddings into the database:** Next, insert the generated vector embeddings into the vector database. It is critical to preserve

references to the original content used to create these embeddings at this stage.

3. **Query the database:** When an application issues a query, employ the same embedding model to create embeddings for that specific query. These query embeddings are then used to search the vector database for similar embeddings using the similarity metrics described earlier. Remember, similar embeddings will be associated with the original content used to create them.

By following this process, we can retrieve the raw data from the vector database that is most relevant to the query. However, this raw data may not be in a suitable format for immediate presentation to the individual making the query. Therefore, the next step in the process involves transforming and inputting the data into an LLM to further refine and generate a more natural output.

Step 4: Input Search Results into LLMs

Let's open this section by pondering a common scenario in day-to-day life. You intend to purchase a product online. What factors influence your decision to make a purchase or pass on buying it?

Interestingly, most tend to bypass the extensive information companies provide on their websites and turn to online reviews. These reviews could be written by strangers who lack professional expertise or authoritative knowledge. Yet, the average person will still rely on the latter for information. This counterintuitive behaviour prompts the question: Why do we trust the perspectives of unknown individuals more than a company's meticulously curated content?

Generative AI has undoubtedly brought about a significant shift in how we consume information. From absorbing lengthy articles to craving concise and synthesised information, much like easily digestible summaries – this evolution aligns with our innate human instincts, prioritising efficiency, conciseness and relevancy.

As we delve into Step 4 of the technical implementation framework, which we have highlighted in Figure 4.9 – Inputting Search Results into LLMs – it is worthwhile to highlight that this shift in information consumption behaviour isn't a novelty. It is our inherent tendency to seek social proof. Humans are social creatures by nature, so we rely on the actions and opinions of others to determine what is correct. As such, the opinions and experiences of those who have tread on the path before us hold significant

Input Search Results into LLMs

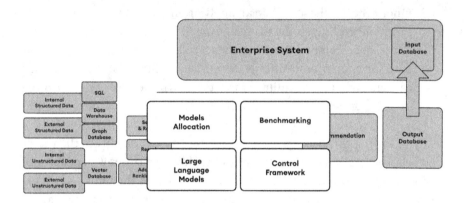

FIGURE 4.9   Third step of the technical implementation framework: Input search results into LLMs.

weight. We find a sense of security and validation in their perspectives, more so than in the polished and potentially biassed information companies present.

Moreover, these reviews typically encapsulate a condensed version of a user's experience, offering us the gist of their feedback without requiring us to delve into a sea of information. Thus, the trend of favouring stranger-authored reviews over company-provided information highlights our preference for summarised, user-generated content over detailed, authoritative data.

It so happens that generative AI intelligently leverages this behavioural trait, which is why inputting search results into LLMs is not merely a technical process but rather a strategic alignment with our innate human behaviour.

Role of LLMs in Data Transformation
LLMs are powerful AI models trained on vast amounts of textual data known as corpus, allowing them to respond to queries in a human-like manner. They combine coherence, relevance and creativity to generate rapid and meaningful responses.

Transitioning from the search and retrieval stage to inputting results into an LLM involves a blend of technical accuracy and human intuition. In Step 3, we may have successfully retrieved material most relevant to a query from the vector database, but it comes in the rawest form of data. To generate concise, easily digestible and human-like answers, we must put the data through an LLM.

Picture a labyrinthine network of structured information within the vector database, representing a wide spectrum of insights, trends and latent connections from the knowledge management system. The intricate process of feeding this refined and condensed information repository into the LLM naturally requires special care and attention to detail. It is why organisations must clearly understand the data extraction's purpose; it ensures that the correct data subsets are filtered and then inputted into the LLM.

How the data transform in the LLM is akin to a metamorphosis. Through its sophisticated understanding of context, syntax, semantics and nuances in human language, it can maintain the integrity of underlying facts and condense information into meaningful, relevant and concise insights. With a feedback loop, the model can learn from its output and constantly improve its summarisation capabilities. This iterative process ensures that we can refine the LLM to keep up with the changing needs and dynamics of the information landscape.

LLMs as Masterful Interpreters

OpenAI's ChatGPT is a well-known example of an LLM that has gained immense popularity. It became the fastest-growing platform in Internet history when it reached 100 million users within two months of its launch in November 2022 (Hu, 2023). Other notable LLMs include Google's PaLM, LaMDA, Gopher and OPT.

All these various models generate likely sequences of data, usually in textual form, based on source inputs called prompts. Whether as brief as a few words or as long as several pages, prompts provide the initial impetus that LLMs require to generate responses.

We liken LLMs to musicians. Present a sheet of music to a musician, and they will learn the piece by understanding its musical style, structure and form to perform their interpretation while staying true to the composer's original intent. Present a prompt to an LLM, and it will learn its intent by grasping nuances, context and patterns to craft relevant responses. A virtuoso provides awe-inspiring musical renditions; likewise, a well-trained LLM is a particularly adept interpreter of human language.

Prompt Engineering

If musicians can be likened to LLMs, then composers are the musical counterparts of prompt engineers. As one of the most prodigious musicians in history, Mozart composed his first symphony at the age of eight. While an exceedingly remarkable feat in itself, his technique and prowess only grew as the years progressed. Much like how a better musical composition produces a more impressive symphony, the effectiveness of an LLM's responses hinges significantly on the quality of the prompts they receive. It is an art that requires meticulous crafting, experimenting and refining of inputs to elicit the desired outputs.

Prompt engineering plays a pivotal role in the generative AI process, as it isn't merely about finding the right words. It is about understanding the nuances of language, the layers of context and the rhythm of conversation that humans innately grasp. It is about steering the LLM towards generating the insights we seek, translating the information we feed into a digestible format that enlightens rather than obscures. After all, LLMs may possess astounding natural capabilities, but they are inevitably constrained by the prompts they receive to some degree.

For that reason, many organisations consider bringing onboard prompt engineers. Given the complexities and subtleties involved, these specialists are trained in the art and science of crafting effective prompts. They understand how to navigate the vast capabilities of an LLM and how to direct it effectively to extract the required information. Moreover, they excel in modifying prompts to guide the LLM in generating more accurate and coherent responses.

The beauty of prompt engineering lies in its interdisciplinary nature. As we strive for diversity of thought and approach, it is beneficial to explore talent from diverse backgrounds. Individuals originally from writing backgrounds, for instance, can bring a fresh perspective. Their deep understanding of narrative structure, storytelling techniques and language subtleties can enhance the quality of prompts, leading to more meaningful and nuanced responses from the LLM.

Let's delve into some examples of prompts and observe the types of responses they generate. Apart from running DDA Labs, Jason is also the host of The Analytics Show, a podcast that brings together business leaders and advanced analytics practitioners. The podcast explores how advanced analytics can be used in modern, high-performing organisations. The entire archive of previous podcast episodes is accessible through a searchable database, allowing listeners to find episodes most relevant to their interests (Tan, n.d.).

Queries from interested visitors potentially include "What episode delves into AI?" or "Which episodes feature prominent female guests?" By utilising similarity metrics as previously described, the vector database can provide the raw data that address those queries. However, it is when we input this data into the LLM that it produces the following responses in natural-sounding, conversational sentences:

QUERY 1: "What episode delves into AI?"

RESPONSE TO QUERY 1: "The episode that delves into AI is E12 – Felix Liao – Deep Dive into the Current and Future World of Artificial Intelligence and Machine Learning."

QUERY 2: "Which episodes feature prominent female guests?"

RESPONSE TO QUERY 2: "The episodes that feature prominent female guests are: 1. E25 – Linda Ginger – On Using Data Science to Engineer Winning Innovations 2. E122 – Kari Jones – Improving Performance & Encouraging Innovation with Data Analytics & Emerging Tech 3. E77 – Geeta Pyne – Insider Secrets to Fast-Paced Agile Data Platform Development."

The examples above highlight the crucial role of LLMs in converting raw data into meaningful and relevant information. Although the raw data can be much more intricate than those illustrations, the combination of LLM training and the right prompts enables the models to produce human-like responses that showcase exceptional levels of creativity.

Approaches for Feeding Search Results into LLMs

When considering the integration of generative AI into workflows, it's important to recognise the diverse range of vendor options available in the market. These vendors offer various solutions, from specialising in different steps of the technical framework to providing end-to-end solutions. Among these myriad possibilities, two main approaches stand out for feeding search results into LLMs.

The first approach is utilising vendor modules, which offer simplicity and ease of use, eliminating the need for extensive coding or technical expertise. The modules act as intermediaries, facilitating communication between the search results and the LLM. Teams seeking quick integration of generative AI without requiring significant time investment will find this approach most viable, but it presents a trade-off between convenience and control.

While the vendor's modules simplify the process, they reduce the transparency of the prompt generation process. It is akin to driving a car with an automatic transmission compared to a manual transmission. With an automatic transmission, the car shifts gears automatically, requiring less effort from the driver. However, this convenience comes at the cost of relinquishing control over gear selection and the ability to finely tune the driving experience.

Similarly, the use of vendor modules simplifies the integration of generative AI but reduces the visibility and control over prompt generation. Striking the right balance between convenience and control is crucial when choosing the approach to feed search results into LLMs. This lack of transparency can create uncertainty around the prompt's quality and its alignment with the desired outcomes.

As for the second approach, we reintroduce a pivotal character in our narrative in the second approach – the prompt engineer. This approach relies on the expertise of a skilled prompt engineer who meticulously crafts prompts for LLMs based on the search results. This process embraces nuances and complexities, resembling an artisanal craft instead of a formulaic procedure.

The beauty of the prompt engineer approach lies in the transparency and control it offers. With a prompt engineer at the helm, we gain precise control over how much of the search result is utilised and how it is integrated into the LLM. The quality of the prompts and, subsequently, the LLM output is in our hands.

The way a prompt engineer carefully selects key elements from the search results, shaping them into an effective prompt that guides the LLM, is analogous to a master chef curating a signature dish by handpicking each key ingredient to create the ultimate flavour profile. This deliberate and intentional process ensures that every aspect of the prompt aligns with the desired objectives.

Similar to a master chef's artistry, prompt engineering is not a quick fix. It requires time, patience and a high degree of skill. Perfecting the prompts and achieving desired results demand a significant investment of time. Additionally, prompt engineers, like sought-after master chefs, come at a premium cost due to their expertise and in-demand skills.

In summary, choosing between the two approaches ultimately depends on an organisation's specific needs, timeline and resources. Do simplicity and speed outweigh control and transparency, or vice versa? Either way, the chosen path will shape how an organisation integrates generative AI into its existing workflow and influence the return on investment from embedding advanced analytics. As we explore further, we will continue to unravel the complexities of generative AI, providing valuable insights to assist in making these critical decisions.

Step 5: Embedding LLM-Generated Recommendations

At the final stage of the process as indicated in Figure 4.10, we should find ourselves with highly relevant and close to accurate outputs from the LLM. With high-quality data, carefully selected similarity metrics and well-crafted prompts, those outputs are achievable.

What remains is to leverage those outputs to transform and improve organisational outcomes. The most straightforward approach is to create another system or website landing page to showcase the generated results.

For instance, "Ask The Analytics Show" is a system that allows users to ask questions about The Analytics Show podcast using the embedded advanced analytics framework (Tan, n.d.).

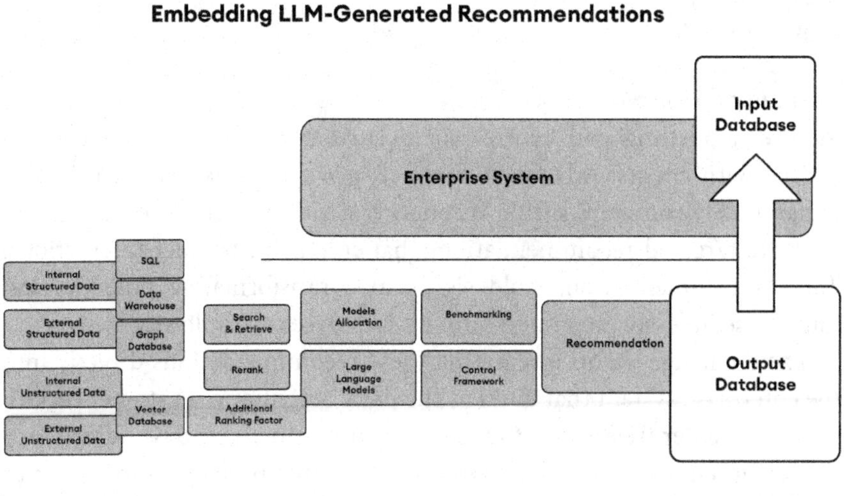

Embedding LLM-Generated Recommendations

FIGURE 4.10   Final step of the technical implementation framework: Embedding outputs from LLM into the Enterprise system database.

While the Ask The Analytics Show system serves its purpose, creating additional systems for frontline staff might not be ideal. Hence, it is worth revisiting the three core principles governing the entire approach to embedded advanced analytics. These principles are particularly relevant at the end of the process, as we now have recommendations or predictions generated by our advanced analytics system.

1. Recommendations and predictions from the analytics systems should seamlessly integrate into existing processes without requiring frontline employees to exert additional effort or interpret complex information.

2. Recommendations and predictions should only update the data in the ERP system's database rather than altering entire processes and workflows.

3. Data scientists and ERP teams should work independently on their respective systems, leveraging their core skill sets and expertise with minimal interference from the other team.

Based on the core principles above, it is crucial to load the outputs or recommendations in the form of data directly into the ES or the system where frontline employees interact. This integration ensures that the recommendations become integral to the enterprise system without imposing additional cognitive loads on frontline employees, as per the first principle.

Illustration: Real-World Use Case

Picture a bustling call centre where customer service representatives engage with clients. Advanced analytics plays a crucial role within this dynamic environment, sifting through vast volumes of customer data to generate targeted recommendations that enhance customer interactions. These recommendations hold significant transformative potential but must be seamlessly integrated into the employees' workflows.

The challenge lies in integrating these recommendations directly into the enterprise system that governs the daily activities of customer service staff. The enterprise system must act as a guiding compass, effortlessly delivering curated recommendations to the employees during customer interactions. This integration creates a symbiotic relationship between the advanced analytics output and frontline employees, magnifying the impact of each interaction.

When the recommendations exist in a separate system, their convenience and effectiveness are lost. Expecting employees to bear the burden of taking additional steps to access them however minute the extra steps may seem, is akin to a conductorless symphony orchestra. Without the conductor to integrate the musical interpretations of the many orchestra players on stage into one bigger picture, the potential for harmony is disrupted, and the opportunity to create a powerful impact is diminished.

Hence, the integration of recommendations directly into the workflow is of paramount importance. This integration serves as the foundation of the technical implementation framework, ensuring that the transition to generative AI is not solely a leap in technology but also organisational effectiveness. The ultimate objective is to orchestrate a harmonious relationship where advanced analytics, ES and human judgement work together, leading to an amplified return on investment in analytics and fully realising the potential of transitioning to generative AI.

Envision a future where call centre agents receive real-time AI-generated insights during live customer interactions. This level of on-the-fly assistance can revolutionise customer service, making each interaction more effective and personalised.

Therefore, the integration of recommendations directly into the workflow is of paramount importance. This integration serves as the cornerstone of the technical implementation framework, ensuring that the transition to generative AI is not merely a technological leap but also a leap in organisational effectiveness. The ultimate goal is to orchestrate a harmonious collaboration among advanced analytics, ES and human judgement. This leads to an enhanced return on analytics investment and realises the full potential of the transition to generative AI.

Integration Points for AI Recommendations

When implementing generative AI recommendations within ES, it is crucial to recognise the key systems and channels that serve as viable platforms for delivering these recommendations to frontline staff. These systems represent essential touchpoints in the daily operations of staff members, making them integral parts of the overall employee workflow.

1. **'Note' section within enterprise systems:** Simple as it may appear, the 'Note' section within ES holds significant potential as a conduit for AI-generated recommendations. By integrating recommendations directly into these notes, we embed actionable insights into the systems that employees interact with most frequently.

2. **Email systems:** As a primary mode of communication, emails often serve as the initial point of contact for customer inquiries. Integrating AI recommendations into email responses enhances the quality of communication, enabling more precise and personalised customer interactions.

3. **Case management systems:** These systems orchestrate various stages of customer interactions, from initial contact to resolution. Embedding AI recommendations directly into these systems streamlines processes, increases efficiency and improves the customer experience.

4. **Business communication systems:** Systems like Microsoft Teams or Salesforce's Slack are central hubs for internal communication and collaboration. Integrating contextual, timely AI recommendations into these platforms enhances team performance, driving better outcomes.

5. **Web and mobile chat applications:** With the proliferation of digital communication channels, these platforms have become a vital touchpoint for customers. Directly feeding AI recommendations into these systems can significantly enhance customer engagement and satisfaction.

In short, the key priority at this stage is to embed advanced analytics as much as possible. In fact, the mantra should be "embed, embed and embed". By integrating recommendations into the channels that govern staff actions, you turn those recommendations into reality. Failure to do so risks wasting the time and effort invested in applying advanced analytics to improve the business.

Conversely, organisations can harness the full potential of generative AI by successfully integrating AI recommendations into ES, transforming theory into practical, everyday operations that drive tangible business benefits.

CHAPTER 5

Ensuring Your Advanced Analytics House Has a Solid Foundation

5.1 INTRODUCTION

In this chapter, we will learn that cutting-edge technology is the tip of a pyramid built on a foundation of healthy data. Although much less sexy than the "cool" analytics, this is a critical part of a successful initiative. Too many advanced analytics initiatives fail because the data scientists spend all their time fixing data issues in Excel before finally giving up and resigning in disgust. We will lay out a basic framework for having your data set up and maintained correctly so you can safely implement an advanced analytics capability on top.

Data Framework Components:

- Data availability
- Data ownership
- Data quality
- Data governance
- Data automation
- Data ethics

DOI: 10.1201/9781003408222-5

We will also point readers to other authors and experts on this topic where they can read further and learn more.

In Section 5.1, chapters one to four, we saw how to create the technology that can enable significantly better decision-making in your organisation. However, this clever new technology is not a magic wand that can deliver success to your organisation overnight, nor should it work in isolation from the rest of the business and its processes and strategies.

5.2 GETTING THE BASICS RIGHT IS KEY

Advanced analytics is the visible tip of an iceberg with the majority of its foundational capability below the water line and out of sight, as shown in Figure 5.1. The success of this technology is spectacular, but unless the foundations are solid, trying to implement advanced decision support is going to be a slow, frustrating and unrewarding process. With the right

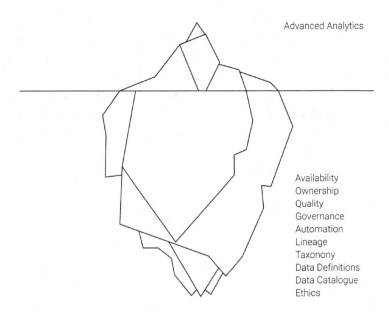

FIGURE 5.1 An iceberg showing advanced analytics as the tip and a large amount of critical foundational components below the surface.

foundations in place then implementing advanced decision support is very achievable.

The tools to build the foundations don't need to be perfect to make a start on advanced analytics solutions, especially early experiments. In practice, it's never possible to achieve perfection or anything near it. The quality of the foundational components will improve as real use cases go into production and gaps and problems are highlighted. This virtuous cycle is what builds the quality of the foundational components over time. Trying to achieve perfection with an early big-bang initiative can result in bloated data quality or master data management initiatives. Many organisations have attempted this approach, often with significant investment over many years, and most are disappointing in what they deliver. I am sure many readers have had the misfortune to be part of something like this. In my experience, the best initiatives to improve foundational data capabilities work iteratively and in parallel with the rest of the organisation maturing in its use of advanced analytics. Thus, the foundational capabilities, the advanced analytics and the organisation all mature concurrently. In particular, this allows the organisation to build an understanding of why the foundational capabilities are critical to success.

I once worked for an organisation in the early 2010s. They were a very large multinational FMCG organisation that launched a substantial master data and data governance initiative worth multiple millions of US dollars. Huge taxonomies were created and everything that could be identified was labelled and defined involving detailed and lengthy semantic debates over the most minor points. These conversations were all happening between data professionals and consultants. Many folks from the rest of the business were invited to contribute, but, as they were unaware of any potential value from the initiative, they didn't prioritise the work. They didn't understand the point of the initiative and couldn't therefore see how it could create value. The project team complained that the rest of the organisation was not supporting the initiative. Millions of dollars were invested in creating hundreds of artefacts; highly detailed definitions emerged that, sadly, never saw the light of day. As soon as they attempted to use any of it, it failed badly. The definitions were esoteric and not fit for purpose because the people who understood the data and the business context had not been included. These were the most in-demand SMEs in the organisation and were needed everywhere so had to ruthlessly prioritise their time. They couldn't be spared for an initiative that had never bothered to explain its value proposition.

The result was millions of dollars wasted and a huge collection of shelfware artefacts. But fortunately, all was not lost. The framework and structure that had been designed were salvageable and used, even though most of the original content was useless. As data objects became required for other projects, the defective definitions were taken out, corrected, updated and ownership assigned. This evolved as required by the rest of the organisation, based on real demand and value. The framework was useful because it gave a place for these decisions and definitions to be recorded in an accessible and searchable place. Otherwise, they would have been buried in various pieces of project documentation and lost. I took a key lesson from this. You need a framework to give structure at the beginning of the foundation building. However, the actual content to populate the framework will emerge over time as the organisation matures and there is real demand.

I have seen this approach work well. I was working at an organisation that took this approach as part of a transformation to a highly automated data-driven customer engagement model. Rather than trying to define everything all at once, this organisation focused on getting one object right as a test. In this case, it was gender as there was a pressing need to update the approach on that data object. This was done using Excel while all the different parts of the process were figured out. Who was the business owner? What was ownership? Did it need a technical owner and, if so, why? What were the object definitions? What were the object value definitions? What did good quality look like? etc. Doing it for real, to solve a real business problem brought focus to what would otherwise have been a theoretical and academic exercise. The outcomes, which were captured in Excel, also provided the initial requirements for implementing a data catalogue and confirmed to everyone involved why one was needed. With the successful implementation of the data catalogue and the maturing in both technical and business knowledge, the solution has continued to scale. Data objects continued to be added organically, each with a real business demand driving definition and adoption.

Another benefit of iterative growth of the foundational capabilities, in parallel to the growth of the advanced analytics, is that you build trust with the rest of the organisation. They need to build their trust in you, the data and the processes. This is hard to do upfront when people don't understand much of what you are describing and have often had bad experiences with technical teams over promising and under delivering in the past. As you deliver success and build capability, the trust in all components of the solution will grow.

One of the key reasons why building foundational capabilities is critical is that AI will automate and accelerate what you have – good or bad. AI will turn your data into outputs for your customers at an unbelievable pace and scale. If you put rubbish in, you will get rubbish out and go on to create chaos for your customers. If you do not build a solid data foundation, you will just make bad decisions faster and more frequently and with a wider reach.

A very relevant and widely known example, where good intent can go horribly wrong if the right foundational steps are not followed, was the Amazons AMZN.O product. This was a tool to help automate and remove human bias from the recruiting process. Unfortunately, because the training data contained bias the tool did the opposite and actually baked the original human bias in and amplified it. In this case, they realised the 10 years of historical data used to train the AI to identify great hires was deeply flawed. It was intrinsically biased due to systemic biases in the tech industry. Historically, the organisation had predominantly hired males from particular demographics therefore all their most successful hires came from those demographics. This circular logic was baked into the AI logic by the training data. So rather than eliminating bias in their process, they inadvertently systematised and entrenched it. This is always a challenge with historical training data as it often doesn't fairly reflect the communities the AI is trying to model. The book "Invisible Women" by Christine Criado Perez provides many excellent, but disturbing, examples of this.

5.3 FOUNDATIONAL DATA CAPABILITIES

So, what are the foundational capabilities that we are talking about? Primarily we are referring to the data, but we also mean the people, the process and the technology. All of these need to work together to ensure the data is in a usable state. If the data is not in a usable form, then your analysts and data scientists will spend most of their time data wrangling rather than constructing advanced analytical models and analyses. This will result in a high turnover of your analysts, machine learning engineers and data scientists. In general, you are going to need data engineers to start building a data foundation ahead of the data scientists and analysts. The foundation does not need to be complete or perfect, but there should be something in place from the start. From there, the foundation can be matured as the advanced analytic capabilities and business experience matures.

This is unfortunately not the sexy activity that garners lots of attention in boardrooms or at conferences, but it is crucial to success. I have seen a number of interesting proofs of concept and proofs of value never go live because there was no sustainable data foundation to move them on to. Even worse is where things do go live but the AI or ML is using poor quality data with often disastrous results. The speed and scale of AI/ML apply equally to poor decision-making, as good decision-making, so it is important to have the right "data fuel" for the engines.

Figure 5.2 shows a simple framework that I have evolved over time to provide initial structure. There are other more complex ones available and many books have been written on the topic. I strongly recommend Jordan Morrow's book *Be Data Driven* as a good example. All of Morrow's books are well worth reading for those interested in data and analytics.

1. Data availability – Data availability refers to the breadth and depth of data available to an organisation. It is a key input when prioritising a data roadmap. It is useful to do a stock take of what data you have, where it is and how accessible it is. Some data may be locked away in

A Simple Data Foundation Framework

Data availability	Data ownership	Data quality
Data availability refers to what data is available to an organisation, where it is located and how easy it is to access. It is a key input when prioritising a data roadmap.	Data ownership refers to the person who ultimately has authority to make decisions over the use and standards of a particular data object. It is important that they have a thorough understanding of the business context of the decisions the data will support.	Data quality refers to the accuracy, completeness, consistency, and relevance of data. It includes the setting of the standards against which the data quality is measured.

Data governance	Data ethics
Data governance is the set of practices, policies and procedures that organisations put in place to manage their data assets effectively. It involves the creation and enforcement of rules and standards for data management, including data quality, data security and data privacy.	Data ethics refers to the moral principles and values that govern the collection, use and sharing of data. It involves considering the ethical implications of data-related decisions and actions.

FIGURE 5.2   A table showing some key foundational data components.

difficult-to-access applications or organisational silos. A simple list is a good starting point, even if you have limited detail on many of the data sets. You can then prioritise your advanced analytics approach based on the most valuable and accessible data.

2. Data ownership – Data ownership refers to the person who ultimately has authority to make decisions over the use and standards of a particular data object. They must have a thorough understanding of the business context of the decisions the data will support. It is also important that the data is owned by someone outside the data teams. The data is only valuable once it has meaning and context applied. This is only achievable by someone from the operational part of the organisation who understands the business context and the questions that are being answered. Someone who actually makes the decisions the data will support. This in turns means there is a need for data literacy to ensure the data owners have the necessary skills to deliver the definitions and rules the data teams will need. It also means that the data teams should learn the business language of the rest of the organisation and be "business literate".

3. Data quality – Data quality refers to the accuracy, completeness, consistency and relevance of data. Data must be of a suitable quality standard so decision-makers can rely on it, both to support business operations and comply with regulatory requirements. Poor data quality can lead to errors, inconsistencies, and incorrect conclusions. To improve data quality, organisations must establish data quality standards, develop data quality metrics, and implement processes to monitor, assess and improve data quality. This involves data profiling, data cleansing and data enrichment techniques, which aim to identify and correct data errors, gaps and inconsistencies. Ensuring appropriate data quality is an ongoing process requiring continuous monitoring and improvement to maintain the accuracy and relevance of the data. The data owner must define what is an acceptable level of quality for the data. Some simple rules can be applied by the technical team. For example, if a field should be an email address then a simple format template can be applied. But in general, the majority of the most important rules require the business context of the decisions that the data will support to understand the quality rules. The quality of the data can then be measured against the criteria and the health of the data tracked. Simple metrics like how

many customer records have a valid email address can be a useful starting point. To learn more about data quality and in particular data cleansing I would recommend "Between the Spreadsheets" by Susan Walsh.

4. Data governance – Data governance is the set of practices, policies and procedures organisations put in place to manage data assets effectively. It involves the creation and enforcement of rules and standards for data management, including data quality, data security and data privacy. Data governance ensures data is accurate, consistent, and accessible to those who need it while maintaining its confidentiality and protecting it from unauthorised access or misuse. It also involves defining roles and responsibilities for data management, establishing processes for data collection, storage and use, and providing training and guidance for employees who handle data. Effective data governance can help organisations maximise the value of their data assets and minimise the risks associated with data management.

5. Ethics – Data ethics refers to the moral principles and values that govern the collection, use and sharing of data. It involves considering the ethical implications of data-related decisions and actions, including data privacy, security and fairness. Data ethics recognises that data can impact individuals, society and the environment, and responsible data practices should consider these impacts. Ethical considerations in data use can include issues such as data bias, discrimination and the protection of sensitive personal information. Ethical data practices aim to ensure that data is collected, used and shared in ways that are respectful, transparent and fair to all stakeholders. Establishing data ethics guidelines and policies can help organisations make ethical decisions and promote trust and transparency in their use of data. We have a separate section discussing data ethics in Chapter 13. This needs to be a part of any data framework, at least as a placeholder, so you can start having the right conversations.

A good example of how seemingly simple data questions can get complex very quickly. The CEO of a large retail organisation asks how many stores they have. They seem to get different answers from all of their GMs. The reason is that the answer depends on context and what decision you are making. Do you mean only stores the company owns? Does it include leased properties? Does it include franchise stores that are actually legally part of another company? Does it include a "pop-up" store within another store? Different GMs have different store numbers because they are using the data to answer different questions. Clear ownership and governance can ensure the different lenses on the data concept of "store" have different labels, definitions and data quality rules. Technical team members are unlikely to be aware of all the contextual subtleties, but they can have a huge impact on the values and the business decisions being made.

Automation is your friend in building and maintaining your data foundation. AI and machine learning tools are not only for the cool front end, user-facing, applications. They are also very powerful tools to automate backend data processes. There are many applications on the market now from vendors that will partially or fully automate functions such as generating data quality rules, generating data lineage, monitoring data quality, initiating basic load repairs, monitoring scheduling etc. Smart use of this technology can massively accelerate your advanced analytics programme and reduce the cost of running it. In addition, because computers are excellent at boring repetitive tasks, when used wisely they can maintain the health of your data more effectively (and cheaper) than human beings. Furthermore, the latest technologies can actually improve your data quality autonomously. This frees up your people to work on interesting analytical tasks.

CHAPTER 6

Understand Your Business – Moments That Matter

6.1 INTRODUCTION

In this chapter, we will learn that we must not assume we know better than our colleagues in terms of what they need. We will also learn not to rely on believing that if we build a great solution they will come and use it. Too many advanced analytics initiatives end up as shelfware or never get past the proof-of-concept (PoC) or proof-of-value (PoV) stage because they don't have a clear business purpose or value. Funding may have been secured to kick things off, but there will be no support to roll it out or for its ongoing use if the rest of the organisation doesn't understand how they can get value from it.

6.2 DO NOT START BY "SELLING" YOUR IDEAS

It's important to stay well away from taking a "build it and they will come approach". Do not "sell" your product. You need to build partnerships in your organisation with your peers and other business unit leaders. In our experience, any attempt at "selling" a strategy to the rest of the organisation is almost certainly doomed to fail. People know when they are being sold to and know that infers you are putting your own interests ahead of theirs. This naturally puts people on the defensive and builds a culture of challenge and negotiation rather than partnership and cooperation.

 DOI: 10.1201/9781003408222-6

If you ask for people's priorities, but you already have an outcome in mind, then you are only going to use that information to attempt to manipulate them into supporting your predetermined point of view. I strongly advise against doing this; it's easy to spot and is likely to backfire. Even if you get enough support to have an initiative approved, it will rapidly evaporate when challenges occur or budgets are squeezed. We have seen that a much better approach is to work backwards from the business strategy and your peers' priorities without any preconceived ideas of how to use advanced analytics to support the overall strategy. This way, your advanced analytics capabilities become key enablers for business outcomes, rather than orphans that struggle for lack of broad support.

6.3 FIRST SEEK TO UNDERSTAND HOW YOUR ORGANISATION DELIVERS VALUE

This all boils down to getting to know your organisation first before leaping to conclusions about how to implement the technology. A good first step is to build a deep understanding of how your business makes money (or delivers value if it is a not-for-profit organisation). In the rest of the book, we use language describing for-profit organisations. However, all the points we make are just as relevant to not-for-profits by substituting making money for delivering value or outcomes.

If you don't understand how your organisation delivers value, then you are never going to have credibility in conversations with your peers. It is not always as obvious as it seems to understand how a business delivers value. Often, the simple answer on the surface is not the real answer.

A good illustration is found in some consumer goods retail organisations. Many have a split between the concept of a flagship store, often in very expensive, prime locations, and factory or outlet stores, often in cheaper locations (such as outlet malls). In many organisations, the flagship stores make little or no money and the profit margins on the very high end, premium products are often very low or even non-existent. Counter intuitively, it is the higher volume, more commodity items, sold in the factory stores that generate all the profit. The flagship stores are often considered more of a marketing and brand investment than generating profit in their own right. Any technologist that doesn't understand this will not understand how the rest of the organisation will prioritise investments in a given market context.

The CFO can be your best friend in this. The finance team should be well placed to understand the flow of money in the organisation and should be able to explain exactly where the margin is made that fuels the rest of the organisation. They can explain the way investments are prioritised and managed. This insight can help you understand the parts of the business where technology can make a real difference and where investments are liable to be prioritised. It is also a good place to understand the financial context that the business is operating in now. Is cash conservation the current priority, or is it all about making growth-focused capital investments or improving brand awareness? This is also an opportunity to learn the language that the finance team is using and how they structure and view the organisation. They are almost certainly a key stakeholder in any business case approval for your investments. Being able to speak to them in a language they understand while showing that you clearly understand their context and constraints will help ease the business case process for you.

6.4 GET TO KNOW YOUR PEERS AND COLLEAGUES AND THEIR REALITIES

The next step is to speak with your peers in the organisation. The key to these conversations is that they do most of the talking and you listen, and we mean really listen. There's a big difference between listening to understand and listening to react. Listening to understand means that you put aside what you want to say and turn your full attention to what your peer is saying and then ask follow-up questions to deepen your understanding. You can also periodically check your understanding by playing back what you have heard in your own words. It is not a chance to show off what you think you know or try to "sell" them on some cool technology.

Start by building a deep understanding of how the different parts of the organisation work and what they are doing. It is also a chance to learn as much as possible about the challenges they are facing and the opportunities they are trying to exploit. Ideally, you also discover the constraints stopping them from taking those opportunities. As you hear from your peers, you will start to build a cohesive picture of how the organisation works and where the opportunities and challenges are. The real issues are not always obvious on the surface, so the follow-up questions to build understanding are key. It is also a chance to bring fresh eyes and thinking to problems. Try to identify things that are currently accepted as fact which may actually be improvement opportunities.

Any time you hear things like "that is just how we do things" you should note those as potential future opportunities to be validated and challenged. People often won't identify the opportunities explicitly because they are not clear what technology is capable of unlocking. Don't jump to solution mode with them but do probe to understand why things are the way they are.

An interesting way to approach this can be to understand how your peers and the business unit heads are incentivised, KPId and otherwise motivated. Understanding their opportunities and challenges through the lens of their motivations can be a very useful perspective. In my experience, it is the incentive scheme and performance management framework that drive behaviour and focus in an organisation. Ideally, it should be well aligned with the business strategy, but if it is not, then in our experience, it will be the more powerful motivator and driver of behaviours. For this reason, it is worth spending the time to understand these drivers. This is a very important understanding if the performance management plan is misaligned with strategy or is misaligned across different parts of the organisation. It is better that you are aware of this and can craft your approach accordingly. A lack of awareness in this area can have you blundering in blindly to a mire of organisational politics. If you have a well-aligned approach, you will have a significantly better understanding of where technology can be successfully applied and thus have a higher chance of building support, getting investment and being considered successful. If you choose to seek investment in areas that aren't incentivised, you can at least have your eyes open to the challenges you will face.

6.5 MOMENTS THAT MATTER – YOUR ORGANISATIONS' KEY DECISIONS

Another good lens to understand where technology can positively impact the organisation is through the moments that matter. These are key moments in an organisation when decisions are made which significantly impact the profitability of the organisation. Not all decisions are created equally in an organisation and understanding the key ones can allow you to focus technology on the moments where money is made or lost. For example, an organisation is unlikely to be materially more or less profitable based on choosing a photocopier supplier. However, the weekly decision on which products to discount and by how much can be critical. It is those critical decisions that are worthy of investing time in to see how they can be supported.

Hopefully, the key decisions you identify are also the ones tied to your peers KPIs and the business strategy. These moments are surprisingly often not well understood in many organisations. It can be a useful exercise to health-check the key decisions: Who makes them? When and why are they made? etc. Then analyse them based on what triggers these decisions, what the outputs are, and what data is used. This last point is interesting as it can highlight whether the data is fit for purpose; complete, trusted, available, reliable etc. You can start building an understanding of where advanced analytics may enhance and improve these key decision moments. This can be a useful guide to where you can make the most impact on the business. Figure 6.1 shows some of the dimensions you may choose to use when evaluating the health of a key decision.

Including the right data is particularly important and that has a number of its own dimensions to evaluate. Some examples are shown in Figure 6.2.

I saw an example of this when I was working in a large multinational organisation during the early 2000s.

Key product and pricing decisions for the week were made each Monday by a team of senior retail leaders. There were challenges with the data being used by different leaders in this meeting, so it was the ideal opportunity for our data and analytics organisation to look for opportunities to help them. We spent time sitting in and listening to conversations and then health-checking the data on which their decisions were based.

It was a challenging process to track the data back through a web of enterprise systems and individual/team spreadsheets. We eventually found the key decisions were not happening the way senior leaders thought they were.

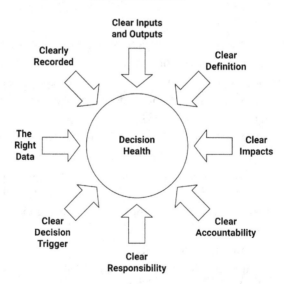

FIGURE 6.1 A circle in the centre represents a decision with eight inward-facing arrows representing the key inputs to analyse and assess the health of the decision.

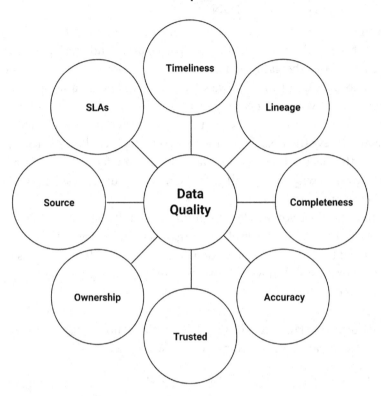

FIGURE 6.2   Eight circles surrounding a larger Central circle, each one representing a dimension to use in assessing the health of a piece of data.

We found discounting decisions were being made by interns and grads in a large complex spreadsheet. These decisions were then validated and tweaked during various meetings throughout the day until they reached the senior leaders as a set of recommendations late in the day. What was interesting was that only the grad/interns had the full set of data supporting them. Any changes throughout the day were being made based mostly on instinct and gut feeling, with some partial data sets to help.

It was a surprise to the senior leaders to find most of their decisions were actually just blind ratifications of decisions made by very junior staff. Once this was understood we could build much more robust data products that allowed all levels to easily consume the same data and validate the previous decisions. Once we had this baseline, we could add advanced analytical models to guide the decision-making and we were ultimately able to automate many of them with a much higher degree of effectiveness.

6.6 BUILD TRUST AND LEARN THE "DIALECT" OF YOUR ORGANISATION

As you spend more time in these conversations you start to build a cohesive picture of the organisation, the pain points and the opportunities. Over and above the gains you make educating yourself, there is another benefit to investing time this way. By listening, understanding and playing back what you have heard, you start to build trust. You walk the talk and demonstrate that you are genuinely interested in working with your peers to achieve their priorities and overcome their challenges. You are not just another technologist swooping in with some fancy tech and a lot of promises who will leave a half-delivered, over-budget mess that will suck up their team's time to sort out.

Something else you will learn is more subtle but equally important. You will learn the local language of your organisation. I am not just referring to jargon, but the particular choice of words which will identify you as someone who understands how the business works. By using the right language, you build credibility with your peers and their leadership. Unfortunately, the converse is also true. You can inadvertently erode your credibility by using the wrong language. Even worse, you may not realise you are doing it. I will share an example from a former workplace.

I worked for a large global retailer in the early 2000s, which had a particular lexicon for the retail locations. They were generally known as "Doors", sometimes as "Stores" but never as "Shops". I saw a colleague from another department making a budget pitch for a technology project to a leadership team. He was struggling to articulate the value of the technology in terms the leadership team could understand, and they were struggling to understand what the technology would do for them.

He lost them when he started saying that this solution would help in the shops. With that one word, he confirmed he hadn't done his homework and didn't understand the way the business ran. He lost credibility and immediately lost his chance to secure any budget. If he had invested a little bit of time upfront getting to know the business, he would have been able to articulate the value clearly in the right language. If he had really done his homework properly, he would have included someone from the relevant business unit the technology was intended for to support pitching alongside him. This would have massively boosted his credibility and likely furthered his cause.

CHAPTER 7

Build Credibility and Trusted Relationships to Unlock Value Opportunities

7.1 INTRODUCTION

The previous chapters have shown you a way to build an understanding of how the organisation delivers value and discover your colleagues' top concerns and opportunities. In this chapter, we show how you can build understanding to create an opportunity to offer your help. This is the chance to show how your expertise can be of value to your colleagues and the wider organisation. They need to understand how you can help deliver their plans and that you care about doing so. You will learn why using the correct language in this process is critical and how to learn it. Based on how your offers to help are received, you can start prioritising opportunities and transforming ideas into initiatives. You will also learn to ensure your partners can clearly articulate the value of what you are doing and why that is important.

7.2 HOW TO START MAKING PROPOSALS

As a result of the fact-finding conversations you have had, you should now understand where the value opportunities are and how to support the key decisions. As you were building this knowledge, you were also building

DOI: 10.1201/9781003408222-7

trust and credibility with your colleagues, and you will be starting to understand where data and technology can make a real impact for the organisation.

You will know that you have reached a key tipping point when your colleagues start asking for your suggestions on how to solve their problems or take advantage of their opportunities. Once you reach this point, you can adjust the balance of the conversations and start suggesting how advanced analytics can add value.

Remember to use the right language and to stay cautious with your commitments. You will be experimenting and not every idea will be successful, so be careful not to over-promise. Over-promising and under-delivering is an ongoing problem in our industry despite good intentions and a genuine belief in the technology. But nothing erodes credibility faster than broken promises and missed commitments. It is a truism that nothing in data analytics is ever as simple as it seems at the outset. You can guarantee there will be unexpected challenges and your partners in other parts of the business must be ready for that reality.

It is essential that you set up your stakeholder partnerships correctly. They need to understand that you are supporting them in delivering their objectives and plans, the potential value that could come from the technology and why this is relevant to them. It is important that they do not see this as them doing you a favour by supporting an initiative they don't really understand the value of. This sort of shallow, superficial support will not last when things get tough. When the initiative runs into the inevitable challenges or there are budget squeezes, you need partners who know the value the technology will deliver and are thus willing to champion it. In my experience, analytics' initiatives whose value cannot be clearly articulated outside the data organisation rarely survive in budget squeezes. They often languish as proofs-of-concept and proofs-of-value that never seem to make it through to actual value delivery. This is the whole point of the engagement model in Chapter 6; to avoid having an orphan project.

7.3 IDENTIFY A GOOD FIRST INITIATIVE

There is an old saying, "Nothing succeeds like success" and there is truth to that. Your first initiative will be the most challenging. Don't take on the most difficult stakeholder or the most challenging initiative first, even if it is of the highest value. Start where you have strong support and a clear business outcome. There must be value, but it doesn't have to be earth-shattering for your first initiative. It is more important to have a business partner who truly believes in the initiative and will stick with it when times are tough. Find a

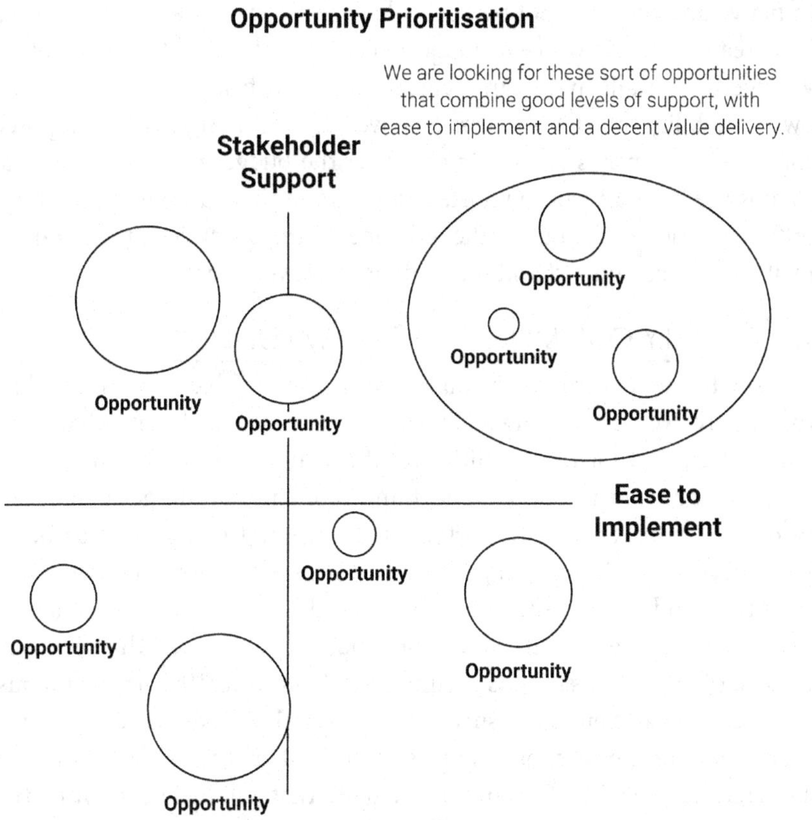

Opportunity Prioritisation

FIGURE 7.1   A matrix showing ease to implement on the *x*-axis and stakeholder support on the *y*-axis. Possible solutions are plotted based on this and those in the top right quadrant represent the best place to start.

problem that has a good balance between difficulty to deliver and the value it will provide. You need to de-risk your first initiative as you have yet to build up credibility with the wider organisation. You want your first to be success- ful and open the door to future initiatives. The matrix in Figure 7.1 is a simple but useful tool to plot the opportunities and identify where you want to start.

A simple test of whether your approach has been successful is if your busi- ness partner can clearly and concisely articulate the business value that your project will deliver to them and the rest of the organisation. If they can't or won't, you will almost certainly not succeed. If they can't, then you need to do more work helping them understand the benefits of the initiative. They must be able to clearly articulate the benefits. If they won't, then you have the wrong partner. This is someone who wants to hide behind you in championing the initiative and they will not be a reliable partner when the going gets tough. Fair-weather friends who encourage you but do not support you are not what you need, especially in the early stages of adoption, before you have built your own credibility through successful delivery. A telling sign is if a supposedly supportive partner is not willing to front the budget request presentation. That is the key moment to register support and share accountability for the initiative's success. If you are the only one asking for budget, then you don't really have their support and they will not have your back.

7.4 CLEARLY COMMUNICATE THE VALUE DELIVERED

The key to the first initiative you deliver is in the value delivered and how that is perceived. Delivering real business value is great, but it will not build you any support for future initiatives if it is not understood and communicated. You want to build support and momentum and get invited back to deliver more. So it is important that engaging with you is associated with successful value delivery. Your peers must prioritise where they spend their time and budget, and you need to build a reputation of being a sound investment partner. Ideally, you want to build a pull model. This means that the rest of the organisation is pulling tasks from you rather than you pushing initiatives at them. Each successful delivery builds demand for the next. That is one of the reasons why it is important that your first outings are successful. They will help build the demand that will fuel future initiatives.

If done correctly, you can rapidly build a solid foundation of support and your key challenge will become managing prioritisation. This is exactly the sort of maturation you want to see. Remember that the focus is always on the delivery of real, measurable business value. It doesn't matter if the solution is technically simple and "unsexy" to start with. It is not the technical elegance or sophistication of the solution that matters; it is the perceived benefit it brings to the organisation and your partner stakeholder in particular.

Your first initiatives are likely to be technically very simple and may not be much more than data cleansing and curating. But if that is the easiest place to add the most value then that is the place to start. The credibility you generate should allow you to mature your solutions and delivery into the future. The highly complex and technically elegant solutions will come later.

We have spoken a lot about delivering value. That is the hard currency to secure future budget support for your advanced analytics initiatives. It is fundamental you think upfront about value definition and measurement with your business partner. This will include socialising and agreeing your proposed value measurement approach with a wider group of stakeholders

Build Credibility and Trusted Relationships ■ 97

to avoid bias. When you come to publish the success of your initiative later, you do not want to be undermined by people challenging the validity of your method. If there are any challenges, they need to be identified, documented and flushed out upfront or you risk losing credibility later. You need to be showing widely accepted success (or otherwise) data after your first experiments if you want to build a solid future foundation for success. You will need to be very clear on the value you are trying to deliver, how it will be measured and what the baseline is. The baseline is particularly key as you can't measure improvement if you don't have a clearly defined and accepted starting point. You must be able to clearly attribute success to your changes, which means work upfront establishing the current position and agreeing on a way to measure, and attribute, changes. Failure to do this has stopped a number of successful projects from progressing because there is no belief they caused the positive impact seen. This is particularly true with very new and poorly understood technology. Figure 7.2 illustrates this situation.

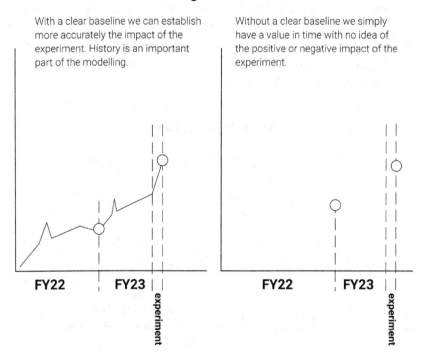

Baselining Your Start Point

With a clear baseline we can establish more accurately the impact of the experiment. History is an important part of the modelling.

Without a clear baseline we simply have a value in time with no idea of the positive or negative impact of the experiment.

FY22   FY23   experiment

FY22   FY23   experiment

FIGURE 7.2   Two graphs Side by Side are shown. The graph on the left shows the impact of an experiment in the context of historical data and the graph on the right shows the experiment data point in isolation with no context to identify its impact.

7.5 AVOIDING GETTING STUCK

I have seen quotes in various articles and publications claiming that between 60% and 90% of advanced analytics proofs-of-concept never make it to production. Although this sounds extraordinary, it matches what I have seen in organisations where I have witnessed it. You can read about the contributing factors in Figure 7.3.

- **Desire for the next bright new shiny thing** – I often see organisations moving onto a new technology before they have finished implementing their current ones. This desire to continuously jump to the next greatest thing means projects aren't delivered and the value is not realised. There is a never-ending cycle of value proving but no value delivering.

- **Over-promising consultancies** – Unfortunately, many consultancies try to win work by massively over-promising what is possible. This builds totally unrealistic expectations with leaders and business stakeholders. These claims are often backed by very fast proof-of-value projects they deliver for free. These are inevitably built on poor technical foundations and are not sustainable. These unrealistic claims can be very damaging to those trying to deliver sustainable advanced analytics initiatives.

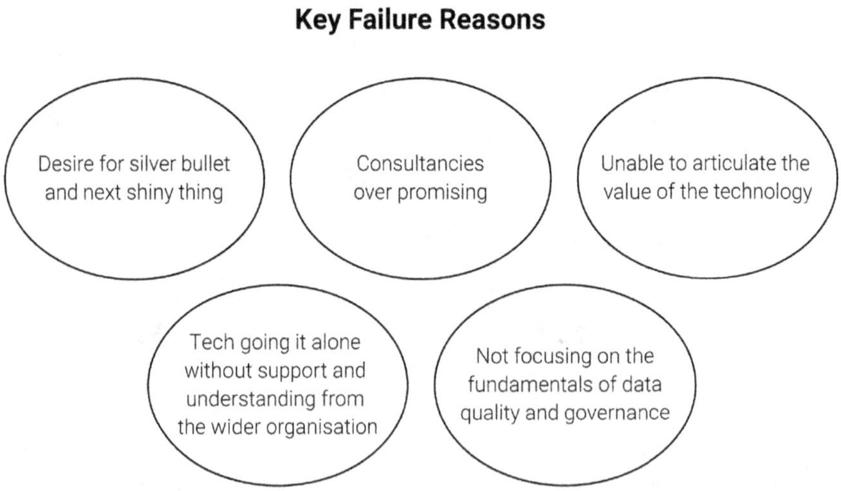

Key Failure Reasons

FIGURE 7.3 This figure shows five common causes why initiatives do not make it to production.

- **Unable to articulate value** – It seems to be common in our industry that leading technologists still struggle to articulate the value of the technology in language that the rest of the organisation can understand. It is impossible to get long-term investment in a technology if the key decision-makers in the organisation don't understand the value it can deliver.

- **Tech going it alone** – The "build it and they will come" mentality still exists. I can count the number of times on one hand where this approach has worked. Generally, when the technical teams implement solutions without the support of the rest of the organisation, they deliver shelfware that will never be used. What makes it even worse is that they will often damage their relationships with the rest of the organisation in the process.

- **Failure to focus on the fundamentals** – Focusing on the data fundamentals first is hard. It is not sexy and often doesn't have an immediate, easily measured, business value. But if the foundation isn't there, the advanced analytics initiatives will not succeed. That said, things don't need to be instantly perfect, just good enough to get started.

CHAPTER 8

Build a Draft Approach and Share It to Build Support

8.1 INTRODUCTION

In this chapter, we start moulding your ideas and opportunities into an approach. The key is co-creating it with your partners, especially those who are actively supporting you. You will learn how to create an approach that, although makes you vulnerable initially, means the end result will be a shared initiative. This has a much higher chance of overcoming any obstacles to finally make it to production. We explore the worth of a principles-based approach and the criticality of focusing on value delivery. You will also learn why you should start your communications planning immediately.

8.2 HAVE A UNIFIED, CO-CREATED STRATEGY

Don't have a separate data strategy – have one business strategy that the entire organisation works towards. You may be surprised to hear this, given how often we hear that we need to have a data strategy. I am not opposed to the rationale that every organisation should have a separate data strategy, but I prefer a slightly nuanced execution.

The challenge I have seen with having a separate data strategy is that data can become a purpose in and of itself, rather than an enabler of delivering business value. This can result in initiatives in a data strategy

 DOI: 10.1201/9781003408222-8

competing for budget with initiatives from other parts of the organisation that should have been enabled by the data work. It is easy for the data strategy to become an opaque and poorly understood set of deliverables that are not supported by the rest of the organisation.

This has been a key failure factor I have seen in several businesses where the data strategy stalls because there is no support from the other parts of the business required to drive it through. In my experience, this support is only resilient and enduring when those other parts of the business embrace the data initiatives as their own and wrap them into their own plans as key enablers. The whole purpose of the approach described in the previous chapters is to build a broad base of support. Using that input to create an independent strategy that causes other parts of the organisation to feel left out, or unable to influence the direction, is counterproductive and will slow or stop progress later. My strong advice is to have a virtual data strategy that is made of the enabling components of the plans of other parts of the business. This includes (the often hard-to-justify foundational components) like data quality and data governance, which can be challenging to create a business case for. These are far easier to support and drive through to fruition when they are being championed by other parts of the organisation which understand that they are key success factors in delivering business value. Your job as a data leader is to articulate those dependencies in ways your peers can understand.

The key is co-create, co-create, co-create. If you want a partnership approach and strong support, then co-create your approach with the peers you need support from. Figure 8.1 shows an approach to achieve this. People are far more likely to actively support and push alongside you if they feel there is a joint plan, rather than merely helping you with something that is seen as yours. This approach can take time to introduce, especially in an organisation with low levels of trust and psychological safety and a fixed mindset. If you are in an organisation like that, don't put yourself at risk. Use this approach where it is safe to, and influence where you can, to mature a growth-mindset culture. Where a growth-mindset is present then this approach will help you succeed. For advanced analytics to truly flourish, organisations need a growth-mindset and a fail-fast culture. If you are in an organisation that doesn't have a culture like that, you are likely to come up against multiple barriers to success when attempting to introduce cutting-edge technology. If you want to learn more about Growth Mindset cultures, I recommend "Mindset: The New Psychology of Success" by Carol S. Dweck.

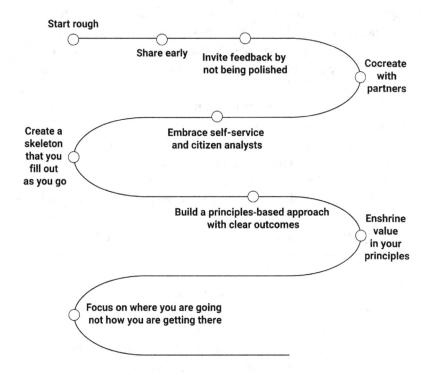

Co-Creation Journey

Start rough

Share early

Invite feedback by
not being polished

Cocreate
with
partners

Create a
skeleton
that you
fill out
as you go

Embrace self-service
and citizen analysts

Build a principles-based approach
with clear outcomes

Enshrine
value
in your
principles

Focus on where you are going
not how you are getting there

FIGURE 8.1   A winding path showing the progression from an initial rough draft through to a formed, principles-based approach.

8.3 SHARE ROUGH DRAFTS EARLY

One of the counterintuitive things I have noticed is that dropping fully prepared documents in front of your peers is not the way to build support and partnership. Sharing a fully prepared and polished document for feedback implicitly suggests that most of the thinking is done, so the scope for real feedback is limited.

This makes it awkward if a colleague wants to share that they think the approach needs to be fundamentally different. My suggestion is to start rough and share early. By sharing a clearly half-finished document (or less) with someone, you send a message that their feedback is welcome and you are still open to making significant changes based on their input. There needs to be enough content that a peer can quickly understand your high-level intent, but the incompleteness is an invitation for them to collaborate with you to solve the challenges and determine the best approach. It is also much easier to give critical feedback on something that is clearly full of gaps and is absolutely not pretending to be complete. It is important to clearly set expectations with this approach (or your peers may be shocked by what appears to be shoddy or half-finished work). You also need to be able to trust the peers you take this approach with. I typically start by jotting down some very rough directional ideas and then seeking high-level feedback. I often just ask for a gut-feeling response. What was their first reaction on reading it? Are they excited by the idea, or does it provoke a strong negative reaction? Keep an open mind with a receptive ear as either is a great conversation starter to unwrap what provoked that feeling. This can then uncover key obstacles or opportunities that you weren't initially aware of.

One of the benefits I have experienced in inviting this sort of early feedback on unpolished content is the opportunity to talk through your thinking with another person. They can help you articulate what you are trying to say. It is often the case that the first explanation you use does not land perfectly or isn't clearly understood. The more you talk it through with people, the more you are able to polish your words to ensure the meaning you intend is the one people receive. I have seen initiatives fail early, not because peers disagreed with what was being proposed but because they misunderstood what was being proposed and hence jumped to the wrong conclusions. This is especially common with new or complex technologies like advanced analytics. By hearing early what people's first reactions are, you get a chance to explain your thinking again in other ways. This can help you clarify whether there is a substantive problem or just a miscommunication. I have found that people are more open and less defensive the earlier they are involved in the creation process. My experience is that people can feel manipulated when asked for this sort of feedback on what is clearly a finished product. If it doesn't look like you are open to changing your approach based on their feedback, then a reasonable assumption is that you only want to hear their objections so you can figure out how to manoeuvre around them. It is not a great way to build trust and support.

The feedback you get from sharing early, half-formed versions of your thinking can evolve into true co-creation. As your partners see their ideas becoming part of the approach and that it is evolving to include their thinking, it stops being "your" approach and starts being "our" approach. This sense of ownership from the co-creation will flow across into the budget requests and the championing of the ideas. No longer are you selling "your" plan. You are co-presenting your shared plan. This is far more powerful and more likely to succeed in the budget prioritisation conversations. It will also make the project far more resilient and much more likely to survive setbacks and challenges during implementation.

8.4 MAKE SPACE FOR OTHERS TO HELP

The co-creation process is also a great moment to learn what resources are available and interested in supporting the advanced analytics journey. There will always be a shortage of analysts and data engineers to realise all of your ambitions. If you don't have enough resources or SMEs, then it may be possible to enable other parts of the business to develop capabilities to support you, at least for some of the more routine or simple tasks. By involving parts of the wider organisation early in defining the approach, you start to uncover future possibilities to upskill non-technical resources and thus massively increase your capability to deliver. I do not like labels such as citizen data scientists, as it suggests a non-technical resource with a limited maths background can replace a fully qualified data scientist. However, the intent is sound, and there are many tasks within the roles of data scientist, analyst and data engineer that can be devolved to non-technical people. This serves the triple purpose of:

- making the technical roles more interesting,
- making the non-technical roles broader and more interesting, and
- massively increasing the delivery capacity.

Another benefit this creates is a deepening bond between the teams. It can remove silos and encourage people to work together much more effectively. The technical teams learn more about value delivery and the non-technical teams learn more about the challenges and constraints (and possibilities) of delivering technology. Synergy is a much-overused term, but this is a great example where working together can bring out the best in both teams, and the whole can be greater than the sum of the parts.

8.5 THINK BIG BUT START SMALL WITH A FRAMEWORK TO GROW INTO

You must remember that you, your teams and the wider organisation will be going on a learning journey implementing advanced analytics. You can read all the books and listen to all the podcasts, but at the end of the day, you need to do it for yourself and be ready to learn along the way. That means making mistakes and taking your first steps without knowing exactly how the journey will end. That is OK, and uncertainty is something you need to become comfortable with. You will not be able to understand and define everything upfront, so starting with a basic outline that you fill out as you go is a very sound methodology. It helps prevent you from getting stuck in "analysis paralysis" upfront, where you waste huge amounts of time trying to define unknowable future activities and returns on investment. The basic skeleton gives you a framework which presents a cohesive, overall pattern to what you are doing, but it doesn't limit you to a rigid, unadaptable structure. Keep it simple to start.

Figure 8.2 shows a basic analytics capability framework. The organisation is only starting with the highlighted capabilities, but there is a structure to grow into as other capabilities are added. This can equally be applied to data models, data taxonomies and governance structures.

8.6 USE A PRINCIPLES-BASED APPROACH

The second important aspect, especially at the beginning, is to build a principles-based approach with clear outcomes. Rules and standards-based approaches can be very restrictive when trying to navigate complex problems. This is especially true early on in your learning journey when you don't know enough about the end state to define rigid rules. In the next chapter, we will speak more about complex problems and how they differ from other types of problems. There will inevitably be exceptions in a complex environment and these can be very problematic with a rules-based approach. At the very least, they can slow you down when teams encounter problems outside the rules and don't have a decision-making framework that they can apply. When this happens, the problem normally must be escalated to central, senior, leaders who don't have the whole context of the problem. There is a need for front-line teams to spend significant time educating senior leaders on the nature of the problem and why the rules don't apply. In addition, senior leaders are often busy and getting their time is difficult. A good decision with a large delay is the best-case outcome. However, the worst case is when the senior leaders make poor decisions with a large delay because of their lack of context and thus send projects down blind alleys. A principles-based approach, with clearly defined outcomes, means teams understand what is intended and can make decisions to achieve the desired outcomes

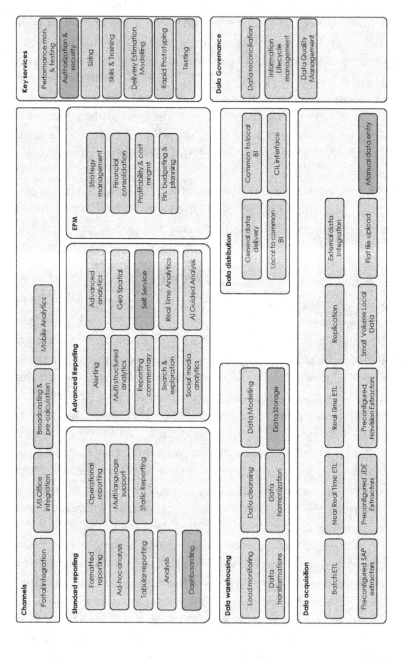

FIGURE 8.2 A framework showing various analytical capabilities grouped by functional area and colour coded to show planned versus those already available.

even in unforeseen circumstances. (Of which there will be many.) This allows teams to keep moving forward, iterating and learning. Major escalations are only needed when a situation is so unusual that the team can't see any solution that aligns with the principles and delivers the desired outcomes.

In Figure 8.3, we see a comparison between a principles-based and a rules-based approach. The difference might seem minor, but it can make major differences in delivery.

While the rules-based approach has admirable intentions, it will run into trouble as soon as an exception is required. And exceptions are always required in a complex, rapidly changing environment. Once you start making exceptions, you need another set of rules to control how exceptions are agreed upon and managed. The alternative is slowing progress to a crawl by stopping all activities that are not 100% compliant with the rules. In my experience, a rigid, rules-based approach is simply not feasible when dealing with complex technology delivery.

Principles vs rules-based approach

Principles	Rules
• We are value driven. • We extract data once and deploy it many times. • We aim for a single version of truth. • We promote Self – Service wherever possible. • We do not copy or move data unnecessarily. • We automate wherever practicable. • We use modular services wherever possible.	• All data will be extracted once to the ingestion layer using the standard ETL pattern and tools. All data must be sourced from the ingestion layer. No other patterns or tooling are to be used. • All data will be held once with a unique definition. There will never be any homonyms or synonyms. • Self-service is to be used to access data. All data will be enabled for self-service access by end users. • No data is ever to be copied. There must be one version of the truth in one place. All information models will build off the single central version.

FIGURE 8.3 A table shows a list of principles on the left and a list of equivalent rules on the right.

8.7 KEEP VALUE AND THE CUSTOMER AT THE CENTRE OF EVERYTHING YOU DO

The most important cornerstone of your approach must be to enshrine value in your principles. There must be measurable business value in everything we do. If not, we will lose support and not be able to get funding or get things into production. This measurable value must be understood and agreed to by the part of the organisation responsible for delivering that value. It is not enough to make empty claims of potential value. Your business partners must also believe in the possible value the initiative is trying to deliver. This does not mean every initiative must have a margin-positive ROI. Value is not just about dollars. It can include gaining knowledge by doing a proofs-of-concept (PoC). But it must be agreed upfront that knowledge is valuable to the organisation, not just interesting. It also means that PoC and experiments can be carefully defined and sized to prove or explore particular areas. This means there should be clear success criteria upfront so the start, finish and success of a PoC can be clearly defined and understood. This stops long, drawn-out PoCs with no clear purpose or value. These sorts of vague, "tech for techs' sake" initiatives seriously undermine your credibility and the trust of your colleagues.

Value is often difficult to clearly define, and that is why it is so important you define it in partnership with the parts of the business that own that value delivery normally. There is nothing wrong with some qualitative measures of success if the input is coming from highly experienced people with a deep understanding of that part of the organisation. Their intuition on potential value from an experiment should not be discounted lightly just because it can't be mathematically modelled and easily quantified. If everything you do as a data professional has a clearly understood, and agreed, potential business value, you are well positioned to be successful.

The last thing in getting your initial approach right is to relentlessly focus on the things that matter. It feels like it shouldn't need saying, but you need to be focused on where you are going and why (i.e., customer, customer, customer) not how you are getting there. At all times, keep your eye on the prize – customer value – and not get distracted by shiny, cool, tech. A fast way to lose support from your business partners is to lose focus on them and their needs by getting distracted and having fun getting cool technology to work.

It is easy to become fixated on the technology and focus on clever solutions and cutting-edge technology. That is a trap to be weary of, as technology is just a means to an end, not an end in and of itself. We want to use the simplest, most cost-effective solution to deliver the value outcomes the customer needs. This means you need to be comfortable pivoting and changing your approach (possibly many times) even in the very early stages of what you are doing. I am surprised how often I see organisations losing track of this key tenet and implementing cool models and advanced analytics tools without a clear understanding of what they will do for the customer. That is a sure-fire path to shelfware and PoC that go nowhere.

CHAPTER 9

Get Started Delivering Value

9.1 INTRODUCTION

In this chapter, we will see how to develop all those great conversations and turn your co-created approach into action. You now understand the organisation and your colleagues, they now understand what you can offer, and you have collectively agreed on an approach. How you get started, and how you frame it up matters, so we will spend some time talking about that.

9.2 SOME BASIC AGILE CONCEPTS AND THE CYNEFIN MODEL

The first thing we need is an agile delivery approach. I'll take a moment to explain what we mean here, as, in my experience, the word "agile" can be quite negatively charged in some situations and requires reflection, research and careful manoeuvring. Here, I am referring to agile with a small a, meaning the adjective referring to a mindset, rather than Agile the noun with a big A referring to one of the packaged delivery methodologies. The agile we are referring to is all about the mindset and the culture, not a particular set of processes. Your organisation needs an approach tailor-made for its needs, not a cut and paste of something that has been transposed from elsewhere.

DOI: 10.1201/9781003408222-9

What is important is that you have a mindset and culture that allows you to get started even when the path to reach the outcomes is not completely clear. This needs a different mentality and set of controls from a traditional monolithic, linear, approach. It is important to tread carefully and to be aware that you may meet resistance if you don't get buy-in from the right parts of the organisation.

Your first steps into advanced analytics are not a good use case for traditional waterfall planning where plans and timelines can be detailed out in advance. With advanced analytics, you need to be learning and adjusting after each step you take. It's a "watch and learn as you go" approach.

It's important that each step in your process is short, defined and delivers measurable outcomes that you can learn from. The learning culture is key because not every step will work as expected and the output may be lessons and knowledge rather than the expected customer benefit you set as an initial goal. The right environment needs to be present so that you can learn and grow. If it is not safe to take small, calculated risks, you will not get the learning you need to mature and grow your advanced analytics capability.

The Cynefin model can be useful to determine the best approaches to problems in your organisation. You can use it to understand why some types of approaches, like waterfall planning, that have previously been successful in your organisation may not be effective for implementing advanced analytics. Waterfall planning is the traditional, linear project planning methodology you would expect to see in a Microsoft project plan. It is very effective for complicated tasks where an upfront analysis can determine the right way to deliver the project to get the desired outcomes. The tasks are planned out in advance and occur sequentially. This approach will not work for complex problems. The Cynefin model in Figure 9.1 explains the different types of problems and suitable approaches to take to solve them.

The Cynefin framework is a model that was developed by Dave Snowden in the late 1990s to help understand and manage complexity. The basic concept is that problems can be grouped by characteristics that then help define the appropriate problem-solving approach. By understanding the type of problem, the appropriate decision-making approach can be brought to bear. The word "Cynefin" is Welsh and can be translated as "habitat" or "correct location". The idea is that you use the framework to find the right home for your problem.

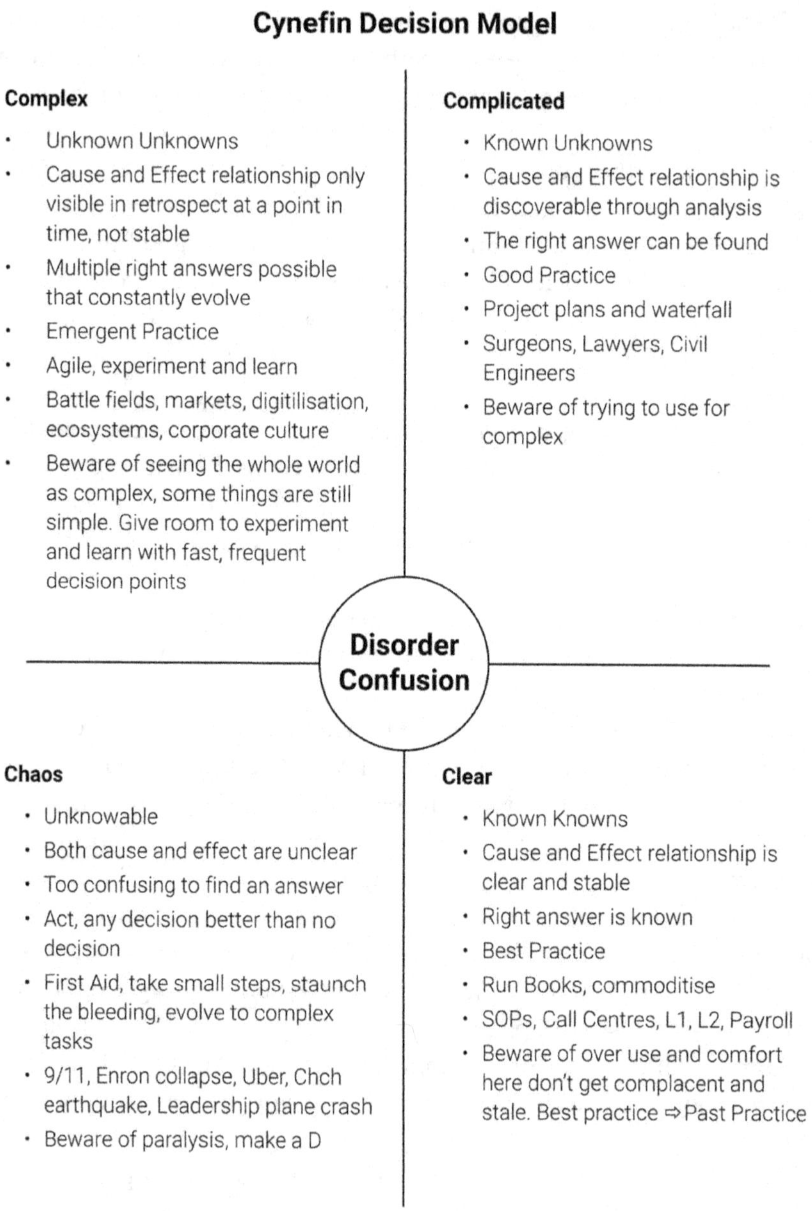

Cynefin Decision Model

Complex

- Unknown Unknowns
- Cause and Effect relationship only visible in retrospect at a point in time, not stable
- Multiple right answers possible that constantly evolve
- Emergent Practice
- Agile, experiment and learn
- Battle fields, markets, digitilisation, ecosystems, corporate culture
- Beware of seeing the whole world as complex, some things are still simple. Give room to experiment and learn with fast, frequent decision points

Complicated

- Known Unknowns
- Cause and Effect relationship is discoverable through analysis
- The right answer can be found
- Good Practice
- Project plans and waterfall
- Surgeons, Lawyers, Civil Engineers
- Beware of trying to use for complex

Disorder Confusion

Chaos

- Unknowable
- Both cause and effect are unclear
- Too confusing to find an answer
- Act, any decision better than no decision
- First Aid, take small steps, staunch the bleeding, evolve to complex tasks
- 9/11, Enron collapse, Uber, Chch earthquake, Leadership plane crash
- Beware of paralysis, make a D

Clear

- Known Knowns
- Cause and Effect relationship is clear and stable
- Right answer is known
- Best Practice
- Run Books, commoditise
- SOPs, Call Centres, L1, L2, Payroll
- Beware of over use and comfort here don't get complacent and stale. Best practice ⇨ Past Practice

FIGURE 9.1   A diagram with four quadrants showing the four different dimensions of the Cynefin model: Clear, complicated, complex and chaotic.

The model divides situations into five areas based on certain criteria, such as complexity:

- Clear – This section is characterised by clear cause-and-effect relationships and problems can be solved by predefined best practices that are widely understood and can be constantly honed and refined. A finance monthly close is an example of a Clear problem. Approaches like Kaizen and continuous improvement are particularly effective here. This is the section of things where we know exactly what we are doing in advance – the "known knowns" (see Figure 9.2).

Knowledge

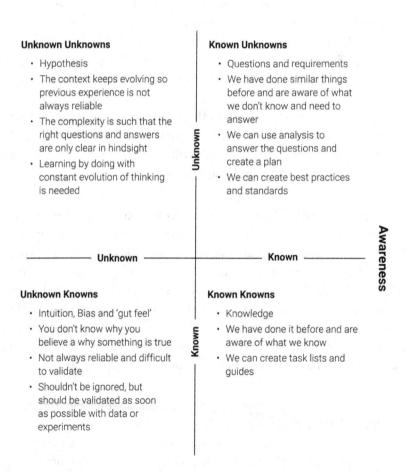

Unknown Unknowns

- Hypothesis
- The context keeps evolving so previous experience is not always reliable
- The complexity is such that the right questions and answers are only clear in hindsight
- Learning by doing with constant evolution of thinking is needed

Known Unknowns

- Questions and requirements
- We have done similar things before and are aware of what we don't know and need to answer
- We can use analysis to answer the questions and create a plan
- We can create best practices and standards

Unknown

——— Unknown ——————— Known ———

Awareness

Unknown Knowns

- Intuition, Bias and 'gut feel'
- You don't know why you believe a why something is true
- Not always reliable and difficult to validate
- Shouldn't be ignored, but should be validated as soon as possible with data or experiments

Known Knowns

- Knowledge
- We have done it before and are aware of what we know
- We can create task lists and guides

Known

FIGURE 9.2 A diagram with four quadrants on the dimensions of awareness and knowledge: known knowns, known unknowns, unknown unknowns and unknown knowns.

- Complicated – In this section, cause-and-effect relationships are not immediately clear, but they can be discovered by analysis upfront, normally by highly skilled experts with access to knowledge from previous examples of similar tasks. Our knowledge gaps are known in advance, and they can be filled in before starting development activity. Building a bridge is an example of a complicated problem. Once we know the space to be bridged, expert analysis can determine the best approach and detailed plans can be made. This is the area where traditional waterfall planning practices are most effective and efficient. This is the area of "known unknowns".

- Complex – In this section, we have complex systems. Complex systems involve a high degree of uncertainty, and cause-and-effect relationships are often only apparent in retrospect. There are many complex moving parts in the system, so it is effectively impossible to build a model or approach that allows full and detailed analysis upfront. The focus for these types of problems is on experimenting and learning through safe-to-fail experiments. Most software development and analytics fall into this type of problem, especially when it is customer-facing. An agile mindset, such as a growth mindset, is essential and agile methodologies like scrum or SAFe (Scaled, Agile, Framework) can be useful if applied appropriately.

This lack of clear visibility can be particularly challenging when it runs into finance approval processes designed around traditional, complicated, waterfall projects. Traditional business cases can be very difficult to define when tackling a complex problem. To be successful in advanced technologies, like advanced analytics, organisations will need to review their business casing processes to ensure they can support an agile approach. If this is not done, then the risk mitigation built into traditional business cases can inadvertently introduce more risk by slowing the organisation down and making it impossible to quickly adopt new technologies.

- Chaotic – Chaotic systems are highly unpredictable and require immediate action to bring them back to a state of order. In this domain, leaders must act quickly and decisively, often relying on intuition and instinct. This is hopefully a rare situation but is typical of black swan events like the pandemic or a major natural disaster.

- Disorder – Situations in which it is unclear which domain a particular issue falls into are said to be in a state of disorder. It is important to quickly assess which domain a situation belongs to in order to determine the appropriate response.

The Cynefin framework helps navigate difficult situations by providing a way to understand and categorise them, and by offering guidelines for appropriate action within each section. This can be particularly useful if you are an organisation that has a strong Project Management Office (PMO) function with very rigid waterfall processes to be followed. The model can help explain why that is not the appropriate approach for implementing advanced analytics and can actually be detrimental to success. It is important to note that there is no one right model for all situations. Each type of problem has its own best approach. There is nothing wrong with the waterfall planning approach when it is applied to the appropriate problems. It is, in fact, the best practice approach for those problems. Likewise, an agile methodology (as distinct from an agile mindset) is not the answer to everything. It is not the most efficient process to tackle a complicated problem.

If you would like to read more about the Cynefin model, I recommend "Cynefin: Weaving Sense-Making into the Fabric of Our World" by Dave Snowden and Mary Boone.

9.3 EVOLVING YOUR PEOPLE AND PROCESS IN PARALLEL TO THE TECHNOLOGY

It is important that the close partnership you created with your colleagues throughout the rest of the organisation, while forming the approach, continues as you start delivering. The rest of the organisation will need to develop and evolve their skills and capabilities to leverage the new technologies in parallel with their development.

This is often slower and more challenging than developing the technology itself, but if you aren't evolving your people and processes at the same time then you are not going to get the most from the new technology. I have seen complex modelling tools ending up as data feeds to old spreadsheets because the wider organisation didn't understand what had been delivered, or why. You built a strong partnership when you created the approach. Keep that going now through the delivery. It all relies on good understanding, good communication and, therefore, good relationships.

Everything must be done in parallel – both the delivery of technology and the maturation of the processes and the people who will use the technology. This is where a data literacy programme is a particularly important foundational component.

In a large global retailer I worked for in the early 2000s, I saw a very good pricing model sitting idle because it had been dropped into business teams without any understanding or support for them to use it. They did not have the data literacy maturity to understand it or the processes to take advantage of it. I saw a far more effective approach in the same team that started with an embedded data scientist solving data quality problems in trading spreadsheets. This grew over time into a complex model that used online customer behaviour to make in-store stocking predictions. This model grew in size and complexity as the business maturity grew and the questions they were asking the model became more and more sophisticated. By growing the model complexity in parallel to the requirements of the team using it, we experienced a large measure of sustainable success. This approach also built our data and analytics team's knowledge of the wider business operations, which also made our technology delivery more effective.

9.4 FAIL-FAST CULTURE

For this approach to succeed, it is important to have a fail-fast culture in place. This is related to an agile, growth mindset, culture. A fail-fast culture is one in which organisations encourage experimentation and are willing to take calculated risks, with the understanding that failure is an inevitable part of the innovation process. In such a culture, the focus is not on avoiding failure at all costs, but rather on learning quickly from failures and using that knowledge to improve future efforts. This approach allows organisations to be more agile, adaptable and innovative, which is crucial in today's fast-paced, rapidly changing business environment. This is especially true when implementing advanced analytics, especially when they are customer-facing.

I'm going to use the "pets versus livestock" analogy to illustrate the importance of a fail-fast culture. In this analogy, pets are projects that are given individual names, personalities and close attention, while livestock are raised in larger numbers and are expected to be more disposable. The analogy suggests that organisations should treat their projects more like livestock than pets, meaning that they should be willing to "kill off" projects that are not working quickly and move on to new ideas.

The analogy highlights the importance of being able to quickly identify and discard failing projects, rather than investing time and resources into something that may not ultimately succeed. By embracing a fail-fast culture, organisations can avoid the sunk-cost fallacy, which can lead to a reluctance to abandon failing projects simply because they have already invested time and resources into them. It is also important to avoid large vanity projects which become associated with individuals and sometimes their legacies. These projects risk being defended, and invested in, even if they no longer make sense.

In summary, a fail-fast culture is important because it encourages organisations to learn from their failures, be more agile and avoid the sunk-cost fallacy. It is important that organisations do not put huge business case barriers and other red-tape in the way of innovation or experimentation. If the barriers to trying something new are too high, then stakeholders will be unwilling and even afraid to allow their projects to fail fast and be killed off. If starting a new project is a colossal amount of effort, people will fight to keep it going even when it doesn't make sense for the business to do so. This is not suggesting that we don't need business cases or governance, quite the opposite. It is suggesting that the governance must be appropriately sized and fit for purpose.

For more detail on nurturing a fail-fast culture, I recommend "The Lean Startup" by Eric Ries.

9.5 THE IMPORTANCE OF CLEAR COMMUNICATION

Effective communication is crucial to the success of any technology project, and this includes both external communication with clients and stakeholders, as well as internal communication within the project team. Good, open, internal communication is essential for ensuring that team members are aligned on goals, priorities and timelines. It is also useful for identifying and addressing potential issues before they become major roadblocks to project delivery.

One of the main reasons why internal communication is so important in software project delivery is that software development is inherently complex, with many different moving parts and dependencies. Without effective communication, team members may be working on different assumptions, leading to confusion, duplication of effort or even conflicting priorities. By maintaining open lines of communication and fostering a culture of collaboration, team members can work together more effectively and avoid these pitfalls. It is also key to ensuring that the wider business partners are aware of wins, challenges and overall progress so they stay engaged and enthused. It is essential that this communication is done in non-technical language that stays focused on the value outcomes, not the interesting technical details.

Additionally, internal communication is essential for maintaining team morale and motivation, which can be a key factor in project success. When team members feel that they are part of a cohesive, supportive team that values their contributions, they are more likely to be engaged and committed to the project and to go above and beyond to deliver high-quality results. This applies equally to the wider stakeholders. Regular doses of progress help keep up the enthusiasm for the project. It is easy to become invisible and for support to erode if you travel in silence.

Communication is an extremely important topic and success factor, so we are going to devote a whole chapter to it in Chapter 10.

9.6 START SMALL WITH REALISTIC EXPECTATIONS

It is important to start your delivery small, add value and then build up from there in short iterative steps. Each step should add something usable to the business/customer and be a discrete increase in value delivered. It is crucial to set this expectation with both the delivery team and the wider stakeholders. You do not want your delivery team believing they will be building cutting-edge, mars rover, technology from day one. It is likely the initial deliverables will be relatively simple technically. What matters is that they deliver value. The delivery team must understand this. They should also understand that delivering technical capabilities far ahead of what the rest of the organisation can understand, or use, is not a good use of anyone's time. As we have discussed, technical capability must be built in parallel with the wider organisational maturity to use it. Technologists enjoy seeing their technological developments used. No one likes seeing all their hard work sitting on a shelf unused, so this should be an easy message to land if it is explained correctly.

Likewise, the wider stakeholders must realise they won't be getting seemingly magical levels of capability in the first sprint. The technology industry has a bad habit of over promising and under delivering and we don't want to fall into that trap. We don't want to give the impression that for little or no effort, the rest of the organisation will receive a magic button that not only solves all their problems but also global hunger and achieves world peace. They need to understand that improvements will be real but will be modest and iterative. They will gain momentum over time, but initial effort is required to get things moving and not every step will be successful. Some experiments will only deliver learnings and not immediate value. They also need to understand that their own teams and processes have to invest effort so they mature in parallel with the technology. In my experience, this is often the greatest constraint, so should be well understood upfront.

9.7 THE BENEFITS OF CO-LOCATING THE TEAMS

Ideally, you want to embed your delivery teams in the departments they are delivering the technology to. If you are able to physically co-locate the delivery team in proximity to the end users, you will get a much better result. This is not always possible, but the closer, the better. Even if you can only achieve sitting with them for a day or two a week, it is better than total isolation. Regular calls and meetings are good, but they do not build the connective tissue that working side by side does. This allows the delivery teams to absorb the reality of the environment the end users are operating in. It creates the opportunity for micro questions and micro sharing of progress. This helps build a feel of a unified team rather than tech delivering to the rest of the business. It also allows for the lunch break and water cooler conversations that cannot be replicated in formal meetings.

Even if you are not able to physically co-locate, it is still very important that you share progress often. You need to be iterating fast and keeping your end users and stakeholders constantly up to date with progress. These updates need to show tangible value or recognisable features. They cannot just be code snippets that mean nothing to the audience. As well as keeping end users engaged and enthused, it allows them to constantly guide and adjust delivery. As we described in the Cynefin model, it is impossible to define complete requirements upfront in a complex scenario where everyone involved is learning. This means the end users are learning in parallel with the delivery team and need to keep tuning and adjusting the delivery based on their evolving understanding. Successfully managing this and not getting bogged in an endless series of changes is where an agile delivery methodology like Scrum can be useful.

9.8 THE IMPORTANCE OF MEASURES AND A BASELINE

For all of this to work effectively, measurement is critical. It is essential to be able to measure what is working and what is not, and then reinforce effective initiatives and quickly shut down those that are not. This means the methods of measuring the value delivered have to be agreed upfront by all the stakeholders. This must not only be agreed but truly understood by all the stakeholders. You do not want the measurement approach being questioned or doubted part way through your implementation or you won't be able to prove whether you have been successful or not. Once the success measures have been agreed then you must take a baseline measurement. You will need something to compare to and this must be set before any delivery activity takes place. These measures can sometimes be controversial, so it is essential that they are fully agreed and understood upfront. Once you have the measures agreed and baselined, you can start delivery and measure the effectiveness of the technology. This will allow you to adjust your direction and delivery based on what works and quickly kill off ideas that are ineffective. You want the maximum effort in those areas delivering the greatest value, so it is very important to quickly shut down any poorly performing areas.

I saw a very strong example of this in a large global organisation. The received wisdom was that discounting was one of the levers that could be used to ensure margin targets were hit. The belief was that when volumes and margins were down, discounting could be used to drive volumes and, therefore, margin. Because of the size and complexity of the operating environment and challenges with data quality and availability, this had never been measured and tested but was accepted based on the experience of some very smart, very experienced people. As part of our advanced analytics journey, the Data & Analytics team built their knowledge of the business operating environment. As a result, after a period of time, doubts started growing in the mind of one of the young data scientists. The improvement in the data quality and availability meant that for the first time, this assumption was able to be modelled. His model suggested very strongly this belief was wrong and the increase in volumes could never compensate for the lost margin. This was very confronting for the business teams involved, but the credibility we had built up to date meant we were able to agree measures and run experiments to investigate more fully. Even with the agreed measures and good data, it was still an emotionally charged meeting when the data presented showed the received wisdom was incorrect and had been costing us money. It was finally accepted, though, and by using the modelling capability developed, we were able to save the organisation millions. This result was only possible because of a number of factors:

1. *The trust built up from a partnering approach,*

2. *The business knowledge gained by co-locating the Data & Analytics team,*

3. *The credibility built up from a history of delivering incremental value,*

4. *The measures that were agreed upfront.*

If any one of these weren't present, it is likely that we wouldn't have been able to create the change in belief and deliver millions to the organisation in savings.

CHAPTER 10

Communication, Ethics and Corporate Governance

10.1 INTRODUCTION

There are many great books out there on communication, and we will not attempt to repeat their messages. Instead, in this chapter, we will reiterate the importance of effectively communicating what we are doing and how to go about it. This is an area that the technology industry is often weak in. We often don't share our success and progress with our internal stakeholders in ways they can understand. This lack of communication can contribute to technology only being viewed as a cost and a mysterious activity. To avoid this happening and to ensure that your teams' efforts are valued appropriately by the organisation, we will use this chapter to talk about communication and how it applies to advanced analytics initiatives.

10.2 DOING A GREAT JOB ISN'TENOUGH, YOU NEED A PLAN TO COMMUNICATE IT

In any field, it is crucial to make sure that your hard work doesn't go unnoticed. You may think just doing a great job is enough, but if nobody knows about it, it won't lead to any follow-up or recognition and importantly you

---

DOI: 10.1201/9781003408222-10

won't be viewed as contributing to the organisation's strategic goals. In particular, you will not build the credibility and support to drive through future initiatives. Therefore, it is important to be vocal about your accomplishments and share them with your team and wider stakeholders. This will ensure the value being delivered is seen and the technology is recognised and appreciated. This helps secure future funding, and more importantly, support when initiatives run into challenges, as they inevitably will.

The way you communicate the value you deliver is just as important as the value itself. To own the narrative, you need a well-crafted communications plan that highlights the key successes and accomplishments. At this stage, I would recommend getting to know whoever manages communications in your organisation and working with them to help you. Your communications plan should include different channels and formats to reach various audiences, such as intranet, newsletters, team meetings, leadership meetings and formal presentations. Look for opportunities to build out the success narrative. A solid communications plan ensures that you're in control of how the achievements are perceived and remembered. Figure 10.1 is an example of a very simple communications plan. For larger more complex initiatives with large stakeholder groups, this basic concept can be expanded. Basically, you want to have a plan for who you want to talk to, which channels you will use, when and how often you plan to communicate and the key messages of what you want to say. Two-way communication is very important as is measuring the success and checking for comprehension. As well as formal and planned communications, keep an ear to the ground to observe what people are saying informally, around the water cooler, know who holds power or authority, both formally and informally, and try to influence these people.

Audience	Channel	Frequency	Content
CEO	1:1 meeting	Fortnightly	Highlights and Challenges
COO	1:1 meeting	Weekly	Highlights and Challenges
Senior Leadership Team	Leadership meeting	Quarterly	Status
Whole organisation	All team meeting	Monthly	Highlights
Project Team	Project team meeting	Fortnight	Highlights, Challenges and Shout Outs

FIGURE 10.1   A simple communications plan showing the stakeholders and how and when they will be communicated with.

10.3 KNOW WHO YOUR KEY STAKEHOLDERS ARE AND WHAT THEY CARE ABOUT

When it comes to communicating your successes, stakeholder management is a crucial aspect. You need to identify your stakeholders, including your colleagues, superiors, clients and partners, and understand their needs and expectations. By knowing what they are most interested in, you can tailor your messaging and ensure the accomplishments resonate with them. Make sure you're speaking their language and are relevant and timely. This will help you build stronger relationships and increase your chances of getting support and buy-in for future projects.

To make sure your messaging resonates with your stakeholders, you need to make it relevant to their needs and interests. Instead of trying to show how clever you are by bombarding them with technical details; focus on answering the question of "who cares?" or "so what?"

- Why should they care about your achievements?
- What impact will it have on them or the organisation?

By making your messages relevant and tailored to their needs, you'll be more likely to get their attention and support. Likewise, they should be written in language the audience recognises and understands. As we discussed in Chapter 6, it is key you use the audience's own language when communicating with them. For example, if your organisation talks about doors, not shops or locations, then ensure you use that language. If the organisation's customers are called members, then use that term in your communications.

10.4 BE CLEAR AND CONSISTENT WITH A SIMPLE COMMUNICATION MODEL

When communicating your achievements, it's essential to be clear and consistent. Use plain language and clearly state what you will do, what you're doing, and what you have done. This creates a sense of accountability and transparency, which can increase trust and credibility. By keeping your stakeholders informed at every step, you'll be seen as a reliable and trustworthy team member. This simple model also gets people used to the pattern of your communications and helps build understanding. Figure 10.2 has a simple model that you can use.

10.5 CREATIVITY CAN CUT THROUGH THE NOISE

Finally, to stand out from the noise and get noticed, you need to be creative in how you communicate your achievements. Using video, cartoons, sound bites, or other unconventional formats can help you cut through the

Simple Communication Model

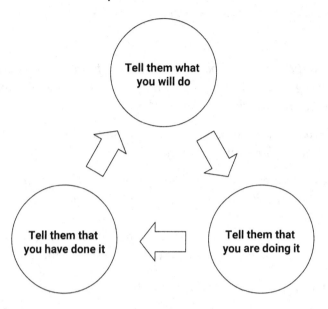

FIGURE 10.2 A simple communications model showing the sequence of communication events.

clutter and grab attention. However, it's important to keep in mind your audience and what format will resonate best with them. By being creative and strategic, you can ensure your successes are seen and celebrated by all. The key message here is that a monthly newsletter by email is unlikely to be sufficient by itself. It is also worth remembering that repetition is important. You don't want to be boring, but the same key messages need to be shared in different ways, in different channels, repeatedly before they will truly "stick". Why is this? We are all overloaded and bombarded by too much information, every day. You need to stand out from the crowd to capture attention.

I saw this done extremely well in an organisation migrating its data centres to the cloud. This large, technically complex project was critical for enabling the future strategy of the organisation. However, cloud in general, and this technology in particular, were not well understood by the non-technical parts of the business. There was an acceptance that it was important but the "why" was not well understood. The leader responsible for the initiative worked closely with the organisation's internal communications team and built a robust education and communication plan to run in tandem with the initiative. This included a variety of channels and approaches with a small number of key messages they wanted to land. The approach worked well and delivered several positive results as follows:

1. *The initiative was supported from start to finish and was understood as being strategically critical to the future of the organisation. It was not seen as a "Tech for tech's sake" project.*

2. *The complexity and risk were well understood by senior leadership and mitigation plans were made accordingly.*

3. *The team received the recognition it deserved which materially helped retention of highly sought-after technical resources.*

So we'll finish this important section by simply saying the following: Communication is key. You will not regret investing effort in this area.

10.6 START TALKING ABOUT ETHICS

This is not a book about data ethics as that is a whole field of study in its own right. In this chapter, we will introduce the topic and explain its importance. This is an entry-level introduction to encourage you to go out and learn more and apply those lessons in your organisation. We will also cover a brief introduction to corporate governance implications.

What is Ethics? Ethics is the study of the moral principles and values that guide human behaviour. It's not simply a set of rules to follow, but rather a framework for making complex decisions in situations where there is no clear answer. At this point, you may be wondering how ethics is even relevant to your work or you may have a theoretical appreciation of its importance in advanced analytics but you may be unsure about how to get started. We hope what we have learned will give you the practical help to get started.

One example of how ethics can be applied in real-world scenarios is the case of an autonomous car crash choice. Imagine an autonomous car is driving down the road and suddenly encounters a situation where it must make a split-second decision. It has a choice to either swerve and hit a group of five adults or crash into a person pushing a pram with a baby in it. In this situation, the car's programming must be able to take into account ethical considerations, such as the value of human life, the autonomy of the passenger, and the responsibility of the manufacturer. These are complex considerations for complex questions that often have no clear right or wrong answer.

So, with a myriad of such hypothetical examples possibly eventuating as you work with and scale your advanced data and analytics, you need to begin now by starting to talk about ethics internally. The first step in implementing data ethics is to start a conversation about it. This means creating an open and honest dialogue about the ethical implications of data use within an organisation. Data ethics should be an ongoing conversation, involving all stakeholders, including data scientists, business leaders and legal and compliance teams. And again, don't forget your communications team if you have one, to impress upon people in the key messages the importance of ethics. You should also start researching what is already being done within your country, your industry and, in particular, if your government has established any frameworks you can leverage. You don't have to reinvent the wheel; we recommend that you take an example and adapt it for your organisation, rather than starting from scratch.

At some point you are going to need to instantiate ethics in your code so your models and AI can make independent ethical choices based on the guidelines and principles you create. An example is the autonomous car we have just talked about. It is going to be difficult, but in order to put ethical considerations into practice, organisations will eventually need to instantiate them in their code. This is a complex task that requires careful thought and planning. The first step in this process is being able to conceptualise and articulate ethical considerations on a whiteboard or in a document. You may get a few key people together in person or online and workshop it through. This will have the added benefit of sharing the responsibility, involving people in a practical task and giving a wider base of people with "skin in the game". By doing so, organisations can create a shared understanding of what ethical considerations are relevant to their specific use cases and develop a plan for how to integrate them into their code. An example might be a situation where you have automated prompts and fulfilment from your website. What if the AI notices large-scale orders coming through from one or both parties in a regional conflict? Will you allow sales to one, both or neither? How will you decide? How will you expect your AI to handle the situation? Suffice it to say, these are considerations to take upfront; AI is programmed and is following your guidance; it cannot do this part for you.

Last but by no means least, this is not a set-and-forget one-off exercise. You need to review your ethical considerations regularly as the environment changes and as you learn from what you have achieved.

10.7 TRANSPARENT AI AND TRUST

Another aspect of ethics and ethical AI is transparent AI. Transparent AI is the practice of making machine learning models explainable and understandable. This is important for ethical reasons, as it allows individuals to understand why certain decisions are being made about them. For example, if a machine-learning model is being used to make hiring decisions, it should be able to explain why certain candidates were selected and why others were not. This not only helps to ensure the decision-making process is fair and non-discriminatory but also helps to build trust in the system. This is particularly critical for being able to explain why certain people weren't extended particular offers, discounts or deals.

Talking about ethics and your values is a way of identifying potential ethical minefields (e.g., inadvertent discrimination against minority communities) before your organisation accidentally stumbles into them. You can imagine that something like this would make a juicy media headline and potentially damage the reputation of your organisation; the very thing you are trying to avoid. We've seen it happen and it is not pretty.

Organisations must identify potential problems that could arise from their use of data. An example of such a problem is unintended discrimination. This can occur when machine learning models are trained on biased data sets, leading to discriminatory outcomes. To avoid this, organisations must ensure their data sets are as diverse and representative of the population they are serving as possible. They must also ensure that their models are regularly audited for bias. This can be challenging, as so much of the historical data we use comes from subsets of university students who signed up to be part of university studies. These are often old data sets from US universities, where the data is heavily skewed towards young Anglo-Saxon males. To gain an understanding of just how prevalent and pervasive this is, I would recommend reading "Invisible Women: Data Bias in a World Designed for Men" by Caroline Criado Perez.

It is important to note that all mathematical models are intrinsically flawed and limited, but they can still be very useful if we understand those limitations and are transparent about them. If organisations are aware of the limitations of their data they can ensure that their decision-making allows for that.

Apart from the fact that all organisations should always be trying to do the right thing by the societies they operate in, trust is another key reason to maintain an ethical stance. Trust is essential when it comes to an organisation's data use. If individuals or society lose trust in an organisation's data practices, it can have significant consequences, including loss of reputation and revenue.

To build and maintain trust, organisations must be transparent about their data practices and take reasonable steps to ensure that they are using data in an ethical and responsible way. As the old saying goes "Trust takes years to build, seconds to break, and forever to repair". It is an essential, intangible asset and must be protected rigorously. The current trajectory of automated decision-making with AI means that organisations need to start thinking about ethics now so they are not caught out later.

10.8 PREPARING FOR WHEN THINGS GO WRONG

That said, even with the best intentions, ethics frameworks and planning, things can go wrong when it comes to data ethics. Organisations must have a crisis-management plan in place to handle any ethical breaches that may occur. Think of it in the same way you will have a Business Continuity Plan in the event of a weather event or a natural disaster, for example. This includes having a clear protocol for reporting and investigating ethical violations, as well as a plan for communicating with stakeholders, such as customers and regulators. Again, this is not something you want to be creating on-the-fly in a crisis situation.

If a crisis arises, make sure your CEO and Communications Manager are informed of the situation in all its detail. Now is not the time for spin or withholding the gory details. Leave the potential responses to your Communications Manager or Media Manager, who is experienced in this field and will collaborate with the CEO and Senior Leadership Team.

You can help here by explaining the situation in plain, factual language and in a calm and frank manner. Any retrospective investigation into the causes can happen later. And remember, it is not about assigning blame anyway. It is better for any external and internal communications responses to be based on full facts so the organisation can deal with the challenge in the best way possible.

Take time out in advance of a problem to war game various scenarios and prepare responses and resources. That type of crisis situation is extremely stressful so it is important everyone knows what part they have to play and what is expected of them. Part of this can be clarity on who is NOT doing things to avoid well-intentioned confusion and chaos. Because everyone generally wants to fix an issue, especially if they are close to the action. Clear crisis response planning is imperative as is testing out your response. Staging a crisis simulation is a great test of your plan. If you would like to learn more about data ethics I would recommend starting with "Data Ethics: The New Competitive Advantage" by Gry Hasselbalch and Pernille Tranberg.

10.9 BOARD CONSIDERATIONS

A related but separate topic is to educate your Board and/or Senior Leadership Team on the implications to corporate governance and risk management of AI, ML and automation. Significant corporate risks can come from an unstructured AI implementation, and they need to be aware of those risks and the right questions they should be asked to inform themselves sufficiently. Some key considerations are considered in Figure 10.3.

Board Considerations

Strategy	Monitoring	Compliance
• Does the board have the right skills? • Does the management team have the right skills? • What Threats does this bring? • What opportunities does this open up? • What are competitors doing? • Is the organisational culture well placed to take advantage of this fast-moving tech? • Is Tech debt slowing you down? • How data literate is the organisation?	• What projects are underway using this tech? • Is there a coordinated programme in place? • How many PoCs are being launched? • How are you measuring value and ROI? • How many PoCs are making it to production and delivering value? • Are you constantly distracted by the next "thing"? • How are you managing bias? • Have you created and tested a crises plan?	• What laws and regulations apply? • Do you have an ethics committee? • Do you have ethics policies in place? • How do you monitor compliance? • Are you able to measure transparency and explainability? • What laws and regulations are being developed? • What is happening internationally with laws and regulation?

FIGURE 10.3 A table showing board considerations for advanced analytics and AI.

CHAPTER 11

Measure, Adjust and Scale

11.1 INTRODUCTION

In this chapter, we will learn how to grow from your initial small-scale deliveries. We will show you how you can safely and sustainably scale within the business unit you have started partnering with. It is important to do this well, as it will form the foundation for scaling more widely across the whole organisation. Many projects end up as victims of their own success by failing to scale sustainably. This can destroy the early credibility they generated by becoming more unreliable as they try to deliver more and more, too quickly. We will learn how to avoid that situation.

11.2 SCALE TO A PULL MODEL FOR DEMAND

Once you have completed your first deliveries and are demonstrating that you can deliver value, you will find that there is a need to keep expanding what is required. One of the benefits of starting small and simple is that there is a lot of scope to add more features and capabilities. You will find as the organisation starts using the basic capabilities they will mature and outgrow them and start asking for more. This is a great situation to be in as you have created demand and it ensures you are building the right things that are valued by the end users. Thus, you are ensuring adoption.

Using this approach, you can build a pull model where the rest of the organisation is pulling capabilities from you and feeding your team the demand. It is important that you nurture this approach and support its growth. It is very important that you don't start to think "you know best"

DOI: 10.1201/9781003408222-11

what the organisation needs and start pushing out what you prioritise. If you do that, there will be no faster way to undermine all the credibility and trust that you have worked so carefully to build up. That is not to say you can't have input into what is being built and delivered. Just remember that you are not the person responsible for delivering value in that area of the business, so you will always need to defer to the business owner who is. After all, it is their neck on the performance chopping block – not yours. As you deliver value, and your credibility grows, you will find that you can exert more influence and will be able to push back more and have more of a say. However, you need to earn your place at the table to do this, so please don't rush into thinking you know best.

I saw this working well in the previous example when the data science team was informing the SVP and his team that their received wisdom on margin management was not correct. Over time and through reliably delivering value, a large amount of credibility and trust had been built up. This meant a relatively junior data scientist was able to challenge the received wisdom of a senior leadership team in their own leadership meeting. This was done successfully, but would not have landed well if it had been attempted too early in the process of building the relationship. Prior to building a solid foundation of trust and an adequate understanding of the business model, this sort of challenge would have ended badly.

11.3 LET THOSE WHO BEST UNDERSTAND THE VALUE MANAGE THE PRIORITISATION

The ideal setup to manage the demand you will be creating is to build a backlog management model run by business owners. In any organisation, resources are always finite. If you are doing your job well, there will always be more demand than there is capacity to deliver it. In my experience, this only gets worse (or better, depending on how you look at it) the more value you deliver. Even if you are scaling your team, it is unlikely that you will keep up with demand. It is important that you don't get caught setting the priorities on your own for the other parts of the business. They will likely try and force you into that position by not engaging directly with each other and trying to play you as a go-between.

Do not allow that to happen!

You need to help your partners to set up a process for collecting demand, defining the value opportunity and then prioritising. You can help to set up the process and even facilitate it, but the partners need to decide the prioritisation between themselves. If they can't decide, then go for a fast, friendly, escalation, but whatever you do, don't allow yourself to become the final arbiter of priority. They own the value of the delivery, not you. You can help and provide input but at the end of the day, the business owners of that area's delivery and budget must make the investment priority calls.

11.4 PROPERLY MANAGED SELF-SERVICE CAN HELP YOU SCALE

One of the ways to mitigate the "resource squeeze" in the highly skilled data and analytics resources is to grow a self-service capability. This can allow you to get increased leverage from your highly skilled resources and is a win-win for the rest of the organisation.

There is always a certain percentage of the tasks the advanced analytics resources do, that don't need their full skillset. If you grow end users in other parts of the organisation to take the less technical tasks, you free up your advanced analytics team to focus on what they love doing and give the rest of the organisation career growth opportunities. This must be done carefully, and in a managed way, as part of your overall data literacy activities. However, when this is done well, it can produce a massive boost to the output of your programme. It will also foster connections between the technical and non-technical teams as well as build understanding across the organisation. If you combine scaling with the appropriate use of off-the-shelf automation tools to help manage your models and data pipelines, you will deliver a sizable productivity boost for your organisation's advanced analytics activities. This can also boost team retention and employee engagement. Win-Win!

11.5 VALUE PRIORITISATION

You will have noticed the word value coming up a lot. It doesn't matter how many models, dashboards or automated decisions you deliver. All that matters is that you are delivering measurable business value. You must ensure that you are always measuring and prioritising by value delivered. This is challenging, but it must be done.

You need to get business owners to commit to value expectations. They will not want to and you will likely need senior leadership support to make it happen. You will need to pre-align the relevant senior leaders. They must be educated upfront on the importance of using value to prioritise and you must set their expectations around how difficult this will be and that you will need their support to force the hard decisions to be taken. You must not allow a culture where the loud voices alone carry the day and set priorities.

At the end of the day, you need demonstrable business value if you want a sustainable funding stream. For that to happen, you need to build a data-driven prioritisation model based on business value. This is always harder the longer it is left, so I suggest grabbing the bull by the horns and making it part of the delivery model from the very beginning. People are already getting used to new things, so it's a good time to introduce the change. Enabling a business owner who can't or won't measure the value of their business area is high-risk and will probably not build you the support base to be successful. Focus on business owners who can and will quantify value and success measurably.

11.6 SCALE STEADILY, NO HOCKEY STICKS

A good practice is to scale steadily and iteratively with small increments. These almost certainly won't go in a straight line, and that is a good thing. As you learn from each delivery, you unearth unexpected opportunities and avenues to explore. This is healthy and should be encouraged. As long as you have value as your compass, you will not be led astray. Do not be seduced by the idea of doing a long-term, big-bang, big-payoff project. Lots of regular little gains are safer and more reliable than placing all your bets on a single initiative. A single big-bang initiative puts all your eggs in one basket, and if that one initiative doesn't deliver, you have lost everything and will struggle to get support for anything else.

Related to the big-bang approach is to be wary of business owners claiming a "hockey stick" business case as shown in Figure 11.1. A hockey stick business case is where there is a long period of big investment followed by a sudden uptick in revenue later. This means that the investment is already made by the time the success can be measured, when it is too late to do anything about it. This is often used by business owners who don't expect to be in the same role by the time the success uptick is due to be delivered. They may be hoping to have moved on by then and thus won't be held accountable to deliver value on the investment. Try, if possible, to focus on opportunities where the potential benefit is immediate and so allow an iterative approach where you can learn what works and what doesn't along the way.

11.7 NOT EVERY INITIATIVE WILL DELIVER AS EXPECTED, TRUST IS A KEY SUCCESS FACTOR

One of the reasons a growth mindset culture is critical is that honesty is key to agile delivery. To be truly successful with advanced analytics, you will need an honest, trusting culture that is comfortable with every bet not

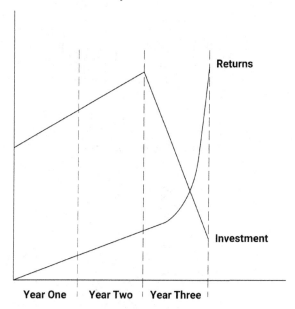

FIGURE 11.1   A chart showing the relationship between investment and returns in a hockey stick business case.

being a winner. If every action always has to have a successful outcome, then there will be no honesty and no learning. It is important to be able to call out things that didn't work so that they can be learned from, and the approach tweaked accordingly. If that culture doesn't exist, then one of three things will happen. Either:

1. People will be too afraid to take any action and will hide behind decision-making committees that cripple delivery speed, or

2. People will be afraid to bet on anything that isn't a certainty. This means that you will fall far behind your competitors as you will only ever implement things they have already done, sometime before, or

3. Your teams will game the numbers and lie about success. Everything will be modelled to look like success, and it will be impossible to identify what is working and what isn't. More time will be spent arguing about success and protecting reputations than in delivery.

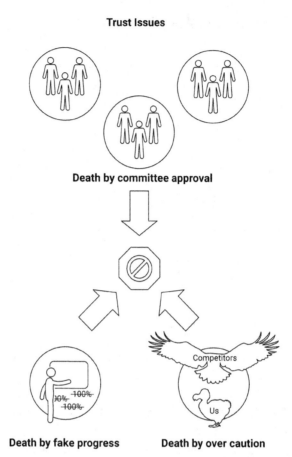

Trust Issues

Death by committee approval

Death by fake progress **Death by over caution**

FIGURE 11.2   A picture shows the different risk pressures that can kill advanced analytics initiatives.

Figure 11.2 shows some of the key risks that can cripple an advanced analytics initiative.

11.8 OBSERVE, ORIENT, DECIDE AND ACT (OODA) LOOP

None of the outcomes we have talked about above are desired outcomes, so a trusting honest culture is key. Good retrospectives help you to continuously learn and improve if they are run well. Success comes when you can take an action, evaluate it, learn from it and then use that lesson to define the next action. This is the basis of the OODA loop shown in Figure 11.3 and why it is a useful tool to use.

OODA Loop

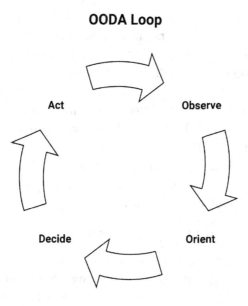

FIGURE 11.3   A circular process flow showing the OODA loop.

The OODA loop is a decision-making framework developed by US Air Force Colonel John Boyd. OODA stands for Observe, Orient, Decide, and Act, and it is designed to help individuals and organisations make rapid decisions in complex and uncertain situations. This is typically the situation in an advanced analytics implementation. The OODA loop can be described as follows:

1. The first step of the OODA loop is to observe the environment and gather information about the situation at hand. This involves using all available sources of information, including data, reports and feedback from others.

2. The second step is to orient oneself to the situation, which involves analysing the information gathered in the observation phase and synthesising it into a coherent picture. This step includes considering one's own biases, values and previous experiences to understand the context of the situation.

3. The third step is to make a decision based on the information and analysis gathered in the observation and orientation phases. This involves choosing a course of action based on the desired outcome and the available resources.

4. The final step is to act on the decision made in the previous step. This involves implementing the chosen course of action and then observing the results to see how effective it is. If the results are not satisfactory, the loop begins again at the observation phase.

The OODA loop is a continuous process, meaning it is not a linear or static model. Rather, its dynamic and iterative approach allows for rapid adaptation and flexibility in response to changing circumstances. The OODA loop has been applied in a wide range of contexts, including military strategy, business management and emergency response and in my experience is a useful model to follow.

11.9 IT IS A MARATHON, NOT A SPRINT

It is important to think of advanced analytics work as a programme of activities with a series of projects. It won't have a finish line as demand will increase as you deliver value. You need to be careful how you communicate this concept early in the process as it can sound like it is a bottomless investment pit with no end. You need to ensure the programme is a series of tightly managed value deliveries with each investment tied to an expected benefit.

Where investments are not delivering as expected they can be quickly turned off or pivoted. It is important you set the expectation that ongoing investment in advanced analytics will be required to counter threats and exploit opportunities in your business environment. The environment you operate in is not static and therefore neither should your advanced analytics capability be.

Your stakeholders need to understand that this is not a one-time investment that gives a single, monolithic solution. Your credibility will soon be eroded if you come back asking stakeholders for more money in the second year when they thought the work was a "once and done" activity. Reliable, ongoing investment is key for a sustainable advanced analytics capability, so ensure stakeholders have the right expectations.

Another key part of a sustainable advanced analytics initiative is to build a support structure for the new capabilities. It is best to build a support structure as you grow to ensure things stay sustainable, rather than leave this as an activity at the end. To keep things running reliably, you will need to ensure resources are reserved to maintain what has already been built. Trust in the new solution will disappear very fast if it is not supported well and becomes unreliable. It is important that a budget is available for this support and that this grows as the capability grows. You also need to ensure there is a budget for scaling. The very first capabilities you build will need to scale as demand grows. It is key for reliability and credibility that you don't allow poorly crafted PoCs into production that will not run well. It can be tempting to rush things into production that look promising, but a build-up of tech debt will rapidly slow your initiative until it is stopped and all your team's time is spent trying to keep poorly implemented technology running. You will need to educate your end users and stakeholders on this before you start so they are aware of this seductive trap and don't fall into it. Starting to think about building out a proper DataOps/MLOps model from your early stages will help. The book "DataOps: The Complete Guide to Data-Driven Operations" by Jesse Anderson could be useful if you want to learn more about DataOps.

I saw this in an organisation I was at. After initially delivering a better trading spreadsheet with improved data quality consistency, this quickly scaled to include some basic predictive models. Initially, this was at a very high level, but there were quick requests to build out the model with additional data and attributes. We quickly outgrew excel and moved into a proper modelling language with a dashboard front end. This was easily integrated by the business teams into their daily processes as they were the ones asking for the new functionality. The complexity and size of the model continued to grow organically based on the demand of the business teams. This resulted in us scaling out the team to deliver more, and we also helped the department setup a prioritisation group to manage the ever-growing backlog of tasks. We also identified team members with an aptitude and interest and started devolving some tasks to them. This grew over time to an integrated and embedded self-service analytics capability in the business team. This allowed us to deliver high-value work, very quickly, with a minimum of friction compared to some other parts of the organisation that had opted for a more siloed approach.

CHAPTER 12

Keep Evolving and Growing

12.1 INTRODUCTION

In this chapter, we will learn how to sustainably scale out from the first business unit we partnered with across the wider organisation. This is where some initiatives come unstuck if they haven't thought about all the variations that might be needed across the wider organisation, like multiple languages and time zones. We will learn here how to avoid some common traps so you can keep scaling and delivering value to the wider organisation. We will also explore the importance of strategic partners, the key role they can play in your success and how best to interact with them.

12.2 SCALING WITHIN THE BUSINESS

Once you have a good system of work running with your first partner and have a steady stream of value delivery, you can look for the next business unit to partner with. I would recommend moving to the next easiest partner to work with. You need to balance the value opportunity with the ease of partnering, but I would definitely advise erring on the easy partner side. Don't stretch yourself too far too soon; stay focused on building your credibility and trust. You will also experience growing pains as you start delivering to multiple teams at different levels of maturity while having to support what you have already built. It is easier to get through the growing pains in an environment that is as supportive as possible.

There is no need to go chasing the business units that are resistant and don't want to embrace the new technologies. Keep focusing on the easiest

DOI: 10.1201/9781003408222-12

partners that give a good balance of partnership and value delivery. In my experience, if you are delivering value, you will start building Fear of Missing Out (FOMO) with the resistant business units. This is particularly true if the early adopters are starting to see exponential value growth (as is quite common) and this is putting pressure on the leaders of other business units. This tends to foster a pull model to scale as other business units see the value and start asking to be part of the backlog. FOMO is your friend in this situation. One of the principles in the early days at Nike was:

"If we do the right things we will make money, damn near automatic";

This could be modified in this context to;

"If we do the right things we will grow demand, damn near automatic".

12.3 SCALABLE ORGANISATIONAL MODELS

Once you are successfully delivering value and scaling up, the real trick is scaling sustainably. It is important you don't allow yourself to scale too fast, even if it is very hard to resist. There are limits to how quickly you can scale a team. Every person you add absorbs capacity from existing members while they are onboarded. Growing the team too fast can disrupt the culture and cause learning to be lost. This can result in poor-quality delivery and fractured relationships with other parts of the organisation. Steady scaled growth is your best option. This will require dedicated focus on people leadership and culture. Don't just assume your top technical people are the best to scale and lead a team or nurture a culture.

Leadership skills are completely distinct from functional skills. They need to be developed separately and not all technical leaders have the desire to be people leaders. Never underestimate the importance of having great leadership supporting your people. There are many different organisational structures, but a matrix model like the one shown in Figure 12.1 can be good for scaling advanced analytics teams. Often called the Spotify model, it is more correctly known as an Agile Scaling Matrix.

This sort of model allows a separation of focus between delivery and people leadership as well as giving technical people a stable home in their chapter, even if they are moving dynamically within delivery squads.

It's important when thinking about scaling to consider all the different dimensions you might need to scale the solution in, so don't allow yourself to grow too fast and fail by losing control. Some of the dimensions you need to think about scaling in are shown in Figure 12.2.

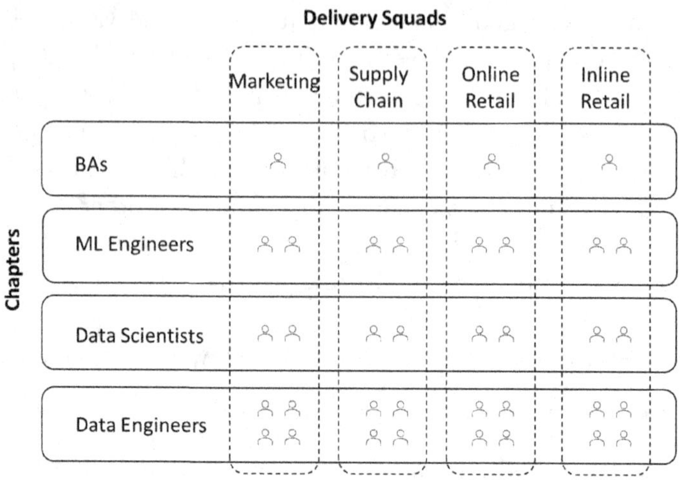

Delivery Squads

Chapters	Marketing	Supply Chain	Online Retail	Inline Retail
BAs	☒	☒	☒	☒
ML Engineers	☒ ☒	☒ ☒	☒ ☒	☒ ☒
Data Scientists	☒ ☒	☒ ☒	☒ ☒	☒ ☒
Data Engineers	☒ ☒ / ☒ ☒	☒ ☒ / ☒ ☒	☒ ☒ / ☒ ☒	☒ ☒ / ☒ ☒

FIGURE 12.1 A table shows an agile-scaling organisational model with functional chapters horizontally and delivery squads vertically.

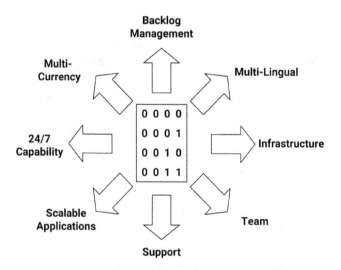

FIGURE 12.2 A picture with a solution in the middle and eight different scaling dimensions as arrows radiating out from it.

12.4 DISTRIBUTED DECISION-MAKING – TAKE POWER TO KNOWLEDGE

One of the key things to support your growth is to have distributed decision-making. A rigid command-and-control decision-making model will almost certainly fail. If every decision has to be passed up a hierarchy and then back down again, your decision-making will be cripplingly slow. There is also a high risk of poor decisions being made as the people making the decisions do not have all the relevant context that the folks working at the coal face have. This tends to mean people at the coal face waste a lot of time writing decision papers trying to communicate context to the decision-makers.

A command-and-control approach will mean your people will probably waste time trying to implement poor decisions made with partial context. And oftentimes, the decision takes so long to make that the window of opportunity has passed anyway. "Command and control" has its place where you have large numbers of junior team members that need a high degree of direction and you accept the trade-offs in speed and agility to mitigate the risk of poor decision-making. But in a highly skilled team, it is not the most effective leadership option and it scales poorly.

It is much more effective if decision-making authority is devolved to those with the knowledge to make the decision as shown in Figure 12.3. Moving power to knowledge rather than knowledge to power. This allows fast, effective decision-making and gives significant competitive advantage. However, it is more difficult to implement. It requires a culture with a high level of trust and an agile, growth mindset. It also needs a highly motivated, well-trained team with skilled "servant leaders" good at communicating outcomes, context and appropriate decision guard rails. This also means leaders must be comfortable having visibility, but not rigid control. The following books can help you understand how to build a culture like this:

- "Turn the Ship Around!" by David Marquet,

- "The Servant as Leader" by Robert K. Greenleaf (and his other follow-up books).

Another downfall of a rigid control model is that it tends to be too slow to deliver, so shadow IT functions spring up to fill the gap. Rather than trying to eliminate this shadow IT function if it exists in your organisation (which is effectively impossible, especially in a large organisation), it is much better to embrace it by building trust and transparency. Building on

Distributed Decision Making

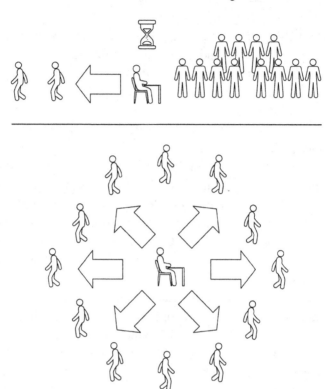

FIGURE 12.3   A picture shows people queueing for decisions in the top half and moving independently in the bottom half.

the partnership you created following the methods described in previous chapters, you can grow a culture of trust and visibility with the wider organisation. You can help guide a transition from unsupportable shadow IT creating tech debt to integrated self-service models that boost throughput and value delivered. This can only happen when you release rigid control and instead influence and guide from a foundation of trust. This is another reason why it is so important to build trust and partnership early.

12.5 STRATEGIC VENDOR PARTNERSHIPS

Good vendors and partners can help a lot in scaling your efforts. With a true, strategic partner to help you scale, you are going to find it much easier. They will have a pool of resources you can call on and high-level experts to guide you at key decision points. They should also have access to processes and best practices they can share with you to help accelerate your journey. In this chapter, we learn how to get the best out of your vendor relationships.

12.6 WHAT SORT OF VENDOR RELATIONSHIP DO YOU WANT?

You need to decide what sort of relationship you want to have with your vendors, both in terms of resources and of software. If it is going to be purely transactional and you will make them invest time and energy fighting for every piece of work they get from you, then don't expect them to commit strategically or invest in your long term.

Even if you are a valuable customer, they know that there is no certainty in a pipeline of work with you, and it is going to be very expensive to submit bids. Their resources will go into preparing and fighting for those bids. If your approach is to constantly fight them on price and always take the lowest bid, then expect to constantly receive the bare minimum of service with frequent trips to the contract to justify change requests.

Your business relationship with your vendors should be respectful, commercially sound and mutually beneficial. If they cannot make money from you and you cannot get value from them, then there is no long-term future in the partnership. In my experience, it is better to build mutually beneficial trusted partnerships. You will need them to lean in and help you when the going gets tough during the projects. If you are purely transactional with them, they will reach for the contract and a change request as soon as they can. You need a mutually beneficial relationship, and it is when that is in balance, I believe you achieve the best results.

One-sided deals aren't sustainable and don't get you through the hard times, as the disadvantaged party will always be looking for a way to exit or reverse the advantage. Building on this, if you keep choosing vendors, project by project, based on the lowest price, you will get what you pay for, and nothing more. There is a reason that the lowest price is the lowest. If you take that approach for the selection, prepare to be gouged later. What I mean here is that all is not what it seems; you get what you pay for and often the lowest price has catches or additions that were artfully disguised or even left out of the original proposal.

12.7 REMEMBER YOUR RELATIONSHIP IS WITH PEOPLE

It seems odd to say, but it is worth remembering that your vendors are people too. In practice, you will not have a relationship with Microsoft, SAP or AWS. They are huge corporate entities with thousands of people.

You will have a relationship with your account team and individuals. They are people – and like all people – they will respond better if treated with respect and as fellow professionals.

If you use periods where the power balance tilts your way to lord it over them, then expect the same in return when the balance shifts (as it always does). Your relationship with your vendor account team is no different from any other relationship you have. If you invest in it and get to know them and their challenges, then you can expect a much better level of support when times get tough or projects hit the rocks and you need help.

With this in mind, I am very sparing with using RFIs and RFPs. These require a colossal amount of effort and investment from vendors. They can be appropriate at times, such as when you are entering a completely new area that is not covered by any of your current vendors. They can also be appropriate for very large, one-off projects where a very formal procurement structure is needed given the quantities of money involved. But outside of those situations, I prefer to enter into close-strategic relationships with a small number of key vendors. This allows me to be very open with them about my plans and in exchange for my commitment; I expect them to invest in terms of resources, knowledge and budget. I have found this approach very effective and it has worked well with the right vendors. The main caveat is the vendor must have the right internal culture. Earlier on in this book, we spent time talking about the culture of your organisation and having a form of agile thinking with a growth mindset. It makes sense to seek out a similar or complementary culture in your vendors' organisations. They need a dynamic, customer-focused culture concentrating on the success and growth of their customers that assumes (rightly) that this will translate into success for them. I have not found this approach effective with vendors still focused on an old-fashioned model of trying to sell their customers as many licenses as possible to build the biggest dependency they can. I avoid dealing with those vendors as much as possible.

12.8 AUTOMATE EVERYWHERE IT MAKES SENSE

Automation is also your friend when trying to scale. The smart use of automation tools can allow you to scale without just adding bodies. This is a careful balance as implementing automation tools, especially off-the-shelf solutions often takes time and capital upfront to set them up safely and make them usable. There is no need for sophisticated solutions upfront so don't waste time and goodwill building a colossal foundation too early. In my experience, it is OK to scale your tooling as you go, as you start

Solution Scaling

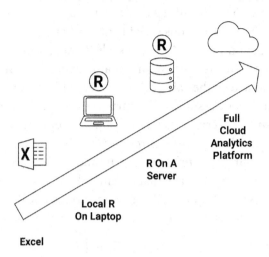

FIGURE 12.4   A flow showing a progression in solution sophistication from excel spreadsheets to full cloud analytics solutions.

outgrowing your initial solutions. An example of this is shown in Figure 12.4. You just need to be careful not to rely on the early solutions for too long so that they hinder progress. If you are constantly looking through a value lens you probably won't go too far wrong.

At one organisation I was at, we started the journey in excel, grew to R on a laptop, then R on a server and finally had a full cloud analytics platform. This progression served us perfectly well and we were able to scale in parallel to the maturing requirements without needing a large upfront business case that would have been very difficult to justify.

It is also critical while scaling not to lose sight of the foundational capabilities you are building on. Don't lose sight of data quality and the other foundational capabilities we discussed in Chapter 5. These need to scale along with your advanced-analytics capabilities and your organisational maturity. It is not a problem if they start in excel as a very first step, but you need to be ready to invest in proper data quality and data cataloguing capabilities quite quickly. These will provide the skeleton and framework you can scale into. If you lose focus on these foundational capabilities, your initiatives will ultimately fail when data quality problems destroy all credibility in the models. Automation is also your friend. There are many good solutions on the market leveraging AI and ML to execute many manual tasks and prepare and curate the data for your teams.

12.9 REMEMBER TO SCALE YOUR COMMUNICATIONS

As you scale up your technical capability, you must also scale up your communications. For all the reasons we laid out in Chapter 10, we need to keep our focus on our communications and scale them accordingly in line with our delivery. This ensures that we maintain support and momentum for the initiatives and keep the value being delivered front and centre with the leadership team. Don't assume other parts of the organisation are as aware of the successful delivery as you are. Complacency can mean awareness fades to the point where your resource and funding are at risk. Ensure you keep focus on your communications plan and scale it accordingly. Your stakeholders are busy and have many demands competing for their time and attention. Without a focused communications effort, your advanced analytics initiative will fade into the background or be taken for granted.

12.10 BRINGING IN THE LATE ADOPTERS

Once you have scaled up to encompass all of your supportive peers and business units, you can turn to any opportunities being blocked by the nay-sayers. In general, I would say to ignore the naysayers and let them be dealt with by the pressure coming from being outperformed by their peers' business units. If, for some reason, there is a need to push and try to get them moving more quickly, then I would recommend using the process we laid out in Chapter 6. Spend time with the blocking leaders and really try to understand why. Not listening to try and convince them, but actually trying to understand their motivations. People always have a reason for what they do. You may think that you understand what their reasons are, but you may be surprised to find that they differ from what you thought they were. If that approach is not successful, and they are blocking major value opportunities, then you will need to escalate. If you are escalating, ensure that you are transparent about what you are doing with the blocking business leader. The escalation should be absolutely focused on the business value being blocked and should not be allowed to become personal or subjective.

12.11 MAINTAIN A FOCUS ON VALUE AND CHALLENGE ASSUMPTIONS

As you scale and grow and become well established in delivering business value, you will build your credibility until you are a trusted partner. Be prepared to push back and expose wastage and bad decision-making as your trust and credibility grow. Start to be a change agent for data-driven decision-making. This can specifically focus on value and how it is measured. You can start championing a data-driven decision-making culture by respectfully challenging and pushing back on unsubstantiated value claims or projections. Ask to see the data, validate where the data has come from and check if assumptions and modelling are being applied correctly. Build a process where value is actively measured after delivery to check the accuracy of estimates. Use retrospectives and the data collected to build a more robust value estimation model to support a better prioritisation model. Do not underestimate the magnitude of this change or how challenging this will be for people. It is worthwhile though, so be patient and keep pushing on it gently.

12.12 RESERVE CAPACITY TO KEEP YOUR DATA AND MODELS HEALTHY

As part of building and scaling your support structure, it is important to remember that models don't automatically stay accurate. You will need to have a solid monitoring and maintenance plan in place. This will take effort and needs to be resourced and budgeted for as part of your support plan. This can become particularly problematic when the volume of data available to the model grows and retraining can take far longer than the initial setup. This is another instance where automation tools are your friend. Setting up a robust and efficient ModelOps process will help you a lot. If you are interested in learning more about ModelOps, I would recommend "ModelOps: Delivering Machine Learning Models that Work" by Dr. Dave Aronson.

In addition, you should reserve capacity to grow your data in depth, breadth and quality as needed. You should not just add data for its own sake, or you add risk and complexity for no reason. Instead, strategically grow by adding data sets that grow the value and versatility of your data. This should happen organically based on business demand, but there are also data sets that other parts of the organisation won't ask for as they don't know they exist or the possibilities they offer. For data sets of that nature, it is the data team's responsibility to be constantly scanning for opportunities and bringing them to the attention of the business owners to prioritise.

12.13 INVESTIGATE IF EMBEDDED ANALYTICS TEAMS WILL WORK FOR YOU

One of the techniques I have found to be very effective when scaling up analytics activities is to look for opportunities to integrate and embed resources directly into the partner business units. This allows your team members to build their knowledge of how the organisation operates and where the opportunities are. It also allows them to build deep bonds with the other business units. This level of engagement can dramatically speed up development and delivery and make the prioritisation process much smoother. Long winded requirements documents can shrink dramatically when the technical resources have so much local context that only very brief notes are required. Likewise, prioritisation is much faster when technical resources have enough context that they can make high-level effort and feasibility estimates on the fly.

On the other side, the business teams learn how to engage smoothly with the technical resources to get the most out of them with the least effort and friction. The Spotify organisational model described above can be very useful here. This model ensures that there is still functional integrity, a career path and knowledge sharing across all technical team members. But it also means their day-to-day delivery is managed close to the business units where the opportunities and problems exist.

I have found it very effective to build from that foundation and blur the boundaries with the other business units operationally. This helps to make data and analytics a well-understood part of everyday life, rather than a slightly intimidating dark art everyone wants but no one fully understands how to use.

I have very effectively used this sort of approach at many organisations where I have led data and analytics functions. There are always challenges to start with, as is always the way in any organisational change, but in all cases, the results have been excellent. Once a fully embedded model is up and running, it can be hard to remember just how much friction and frustration were present previously.

CHAPTER 13

Summary

While there's no doubt that the 2020s will go down in history for the COVID-19 pandemic and ensuing global recession, this decade also marks an exciting moment in time in the world of data and analytics.

Advanced analytics supports organisations by predicting potential risks, evaluating the impact of various scenarios and developing mitigation strategies and contingency plans. It aids in minimising disruptions, protecting assets and navigating regulatory and compliance challenges by monitoring and analysing relevant data to ensure adherence to industry standards and legal requirements.

By embracing these technologies and incorporating them into their business strategies, companies can unlock new avenues for growth, enhance operational efficiency and customer satisfaction. For traditional companies, this may mean investing in modernising their systems and fostering a culture of innovation. For startups, this may involve establishing trust and credibility while continuously refining their offerings based on customer needs and feedback.

As seasoned self-professed data lovers, we are both very excited to be witnessing some truly ground-breaking D+A breakthroughs. Having said that, with great progress comes great responsibility.

We hope our book has offered you some food for thought and some practical tools to help your organisation retain or improve its competitive advantage in the market with clever data analytics. We can't emphasise it enough that there is no one-size-fits-all approach – get to know your organisation and then tailor your approach to fit.

We need to do our best to prepare for and embrace change, harnessing the many opportunities and prioritising which ones are the best to pursue

DOI: 10.1201/9781003408222-13

in collaboration with our key decision-makers. It's about demonstrating that we can help the organisation by getting the right data in front of the right people (decision-makers) at the right time. It is definitely not about having a separate technology strategy, working in a silo or a vacuum, nor is it about inventing impressive tech solutions to try and impress our peers and other colleagues.

In short, success in advanced data and analytics centres on people and relationships. What does great look like? It means staying agile and innovative in a rapidly changing technological landscape, understanding the business we are in, developing our communications and influencing skills, considering our approach to ethical AI principles, having appropriate governance in place and preparing for when things go wrong because they will at some stage no doubt. By upholding these values, we can contribute to a world where advanced analytics and AI are used to create positive change, protect individual rights and foster a more equitable, just and sustainable society.

After all, our responsibility as analytics professionals extends beyond generating revenue for our organisations.

As we look to the future, it is clear that the marriage of large language models and vector databases will continue to push the boundaries of what is possible in AI, data and analytics. By embracing these technological advancements and fostering an environment of continuous learning and innovation, we can unlock the full potential of AI and ensure a brighter, more connected future.

We'll finish by saying that the past, present and future of data, analytics and AI are inextricably linked, with each stage building upon the successes and learnings of its predecessors. As we continue to innovate and explore new frontiers in AI, data and analytics, we must also remember the importance of data governance, privacy and responsible and ethical AI. By doing so, we ensure that the growth and adoption of these technologies lead to positive outcomes for organisations and society at large.

While we live in the age of AI, we must recognise that people are still at the core of any successful system. Even the most advanced AI systems rely on high-quality inputs, calling for dedicated individuals' involvement to ensure data quality. Ultimately, the process has no point unless the higher-quality data and insights generated lead to tangible business improvements. Thus, staff within the organisation are responsible for bridging the gap between analytics-driven insights and the necessary actions for achieving business benefits.

We wish you all the very best with your advanced data and analytics.

Jason and Brian

Index

Note: Locators in *italics* represent figures in the text.

Printed in the United States
by Baker & Taylor Publisher Services